Anne of Cleves

Henry VIII's Unwanted Wife

Anne of Cleves

Henry VIII's Unwanted Wife

Sarah-Beth Watkins

Winchester, UK
Washington, USA

First published by Chronos Books, 2018
Chronos Books is an imprint of John Hunt Publishing Ltd., No. 3 East St., Alresford,
Hampshire SO24 9EE, UK
office1@jhpbooks.net
www.johnhuntpublishing.com

For distributor details and how to order please visit the 'Ordering' section on our website.

ISBN: 978 1 78535 904 0
978 1 78535 905 7 (ebook)
Library of Congress Control Number: 2017960374

A CIP catalogue record for this book is available from the British Library.

Design: Stuart Davies

Printed and bound by CPI Group (UK) Ltd, Croydon, CR0 4YY, UK

We operate a distinctive and ethical publishing philosophy in
all areas of our business, from our global network of authors to
production and worldwide distribution.

Contents

Also by Sarah-Beth Watkins

Lady Katherine Knollys: The Unacknowledged Daughter of King
Henry VIII

The Tudor Brandons: Mary and Charles – Henry VIII's Nearest &
Dearest

Margaret Tudor, Queen of Scots: The Life of King Henry VIII's
Sister

Catherine of Braganza: Charles II's Restoration Queen

Ireland's Suffragettes

Books for Writers:

Telling Life's Tales

Life Coaching for Writers

The Lifestyle Writer

The Writer's Internet

Pastime with good company
I love and shall, until I die.
Grudge who list, but none deny!
So God be pleased, thus live will I.
Henry VIII

Be quiet and merry.
Henry VIII to Anne of Cleves

...my husband hath nevertheless taken and adopted me for his sister
Anne of Cleves to William, Duke of Cleves

Introduction

On a cold wintery day, the king rode with all haste to Rochester anxious to see the woman who would become his next queen. He had heard great reports of the Lady of Cleves and her portrait had shown her to be pleasant enough. Eager to see his bride he spurred on his horse, setting the pace for his five companions. Once he had dressed as Robin Hood to surprise his first wife. This time he was also in disguise because his true love would recognise him, however he appeared. They would fall into each other's arms and love would blossom. He would have sons, fine healthy boys, to continue the Tudor line. The kingdom would rejoice and finally after the turmoil of the past years he would be able to live with his heart's desire.

It seemed an age until they finally arrived. The king strode into the lady's chamber unannounced and soundly embraced the young woman who had been watching a bull-baiting display from her window. Everyone in the room held their breath and then stifled a gasp as Lady Anne courteously removed herself from his grasp with a polite smile. Turning away from this strange man, she resumed watching the activity outside. The king stormed from the room and re-entered dressed in robes of purple velvet, now looking every inch the man he truly was. He was seething inside. His dreams shattered, his heart bereft. He liked her not.

So began Henry VIII's relationship with his fourth wife. The stories of the king's six wives are well-known, covered in many non-fiction books and novels. The old rhyme 'divorced, beheaded, died, divorced, beheaded, survived' reminds us of the fate of each of them. Yet Anne of Cleves stands out as having received less attention than the king's other wives. As I began researching her life – to me, she was the one who survived – a strong, resilient woman who negotiated her way through Henry's reign, that of his son Edward VI and on into Mary I's.

1

As Katherine of Aragon before her, she was a foreign bride. All of Henry's other wives were English. Taken from her home, Anne was plunged into a world she had no concept of and had to swiftly learn its ways, its customs and even its language. My sympathy lies with the many women who were thrust in this way from their comfortable upbringings into the sphere of their husbands. Some managed to have happy relationships, but many more of them didn't.

Katherine of Aragon had married Prince Arthur in 1501 but she was in England for eight years before she married Henry. Anne had mere days. She had very little time to acclimatise to her new surroundings, a sea of unfamiliar faces and a language she could not understand. Where Katherine had known Latin and written to Arthur for over a year before they were married, Anne had had no contact with Henry and language was a barrier. She knew little of her husband and as we have seen would upset him from their very first meeting.

Contemporary reports of Anne are mixed but time has not been kind to her memory. In a book by Sarah Tytler published in 1896, I was shocked to read Anne described as 'a woman of entirely negative characteristics'. The author really had nothing good to say about her. She was 'dull-witted as well as a hard-favoured young woman, possessed of a stolid sluggishness of temper'. Her writing reads as if Anne had personally upset her in some way. She was 'plain and stupid' and even had a 'meaningless expanse of forehead'![1]

She hasn't favoured much better with other authors. Hume described her as 'large, bony and masculine'[2] and Burnet coined the phrase 'Flanders mare'[3] which has stuck to Anne throughout the centuries. Strickland however wrote with more sympathy that Anne 'was a most unfortunate, ill-treated princess...who deserved a better fate than to become the wife of a king so devoid of the feelings of a gentleman as Henry VIII'.[4]

Yet Anne survived him. She was Queen of England for just

over six months and after became the King's 'sister' – a role she adopted and thrived on. She became the richest woman in England for a time with an astounding divorce settlement. Henry may not have wanted her for a wife but he did not blame her for the failure of their marriage – that would fall upon his chief minister. Anne would outlive the king and all of his other wives. This is her story.

Chapter One

Early Days in Cleves
1515–1536

Anna von Julich-Kleve-Berg or Anne of Cleves, as she would be known as Henry VIII's fourth wife, was born on 22 September 1515 in the city palace at Düsseldorf on the east side of the Rhine. She was the second daughter to be born to John III, Duke of Cleves and his wife Maria of Jülich-Berg who had married in 1510 at Castle Burg, a fortified hunting lodge in Solingen, perched high on a mountainous plateau overlooking the River Wupper. A place where Anne would spend much of her childhood playing with her siblings; her elder sister Sybilla, who had been born in 1512, William who would join them in 1516 and Amelia in 1517.

Düsseldorf was then the principal city of Cleves and the seat of the ducal court during winter. Cleves was a small duchy in what is now northwest Germany but was then a state of the Holy Roman Empire although ruled independently. Since 1394 Cleves and the nearby county of Mark had been ruled together but when Anne's father succeeded as Duke of Cleves on her grandfather's death in 1521, through his marriage to her mother, Maria, the states of Jülich and Berg joined with Cleves, Mark and Ravensburgh to make up the United Duchies of Jülich–Cleves–Berg. Thus John III ruled a strategic portion of the Lower Rhine.

Anne had an impressive lineage being descended from Edward I of England and King John II of France and the dukes of Burgundy. Her grandfather John II 'the babymaker', rumoured to have had sixty-three illegitimate children, was the grandson of Maria of Burgundy, sister to Philip the Good and through him Anne was distantly related to the Holy Roman Emperor from 1519, Charles V. John III had a good relationship with Charles accompanying him to England on his visit in 1522 when Henry

4

VIII met his nephew 'with much joy and gladness'.[1]

For all her background, Anne was never meant to marry a king. She was a suitable bride for a duke or a prince but her family never entertained the notion that she would be anything else. Instead she stayed close to her mother 'never from her elbow'[2] and learnt from the matriarch of her family. Her devoutly Catholic mother Maria took charge of Anne's education as she did her other children. William, their only son, would later leave her care to be educated as befit a duke's son but the girls were not seen as needing schooling in anything other than how to be a lady. Anne's time was mostly spent on needlework and embroidery. The only language she learnt to read and write was German. Unlike English ladies, music, singing and dance were not a feature in her education. It was reported 'they take it here in Germany for a rebuke and an occasion of lightness that great ladies should be learned or have any knowledge of music'.[3] But Anne's life wasn't entirely without melody. The Cleves court had an orchestra of musicians and her mother was known to enjoy harp music.

Anne's elder sister Sybilla was betrothed in 1526 at Castle Burg and married John Frederick of Saxony in 9 February 1527 at Torgau on the banks of the Elbe in northwest Germany. Her betrothal portrait by Lucas Cranach shows a beautiful young girl with her auburn hair flowing over her shoulders, adorned with a band of flowers and a luxurious feather. Sybilla would join her husband in his interest of religious reformation in a court with one of the largest libraries in Germany which had harboured Martin Luther after the publication of his *95 Theses* causing controversial religious debate and leading to his papal excommunication. Her husband's uncle Frederick III when elector had founded the University of Wittenberg where Luther taught. When Charles V, Holy Roman Emperor, declared him an outlaw on 25 May 1521, Frederick staged Luther's disappearance and secreted him at Wartburg Castle at Eisenach where he was known only as 'the Knight George' to continue his controversial writings. Luther's teachings remained influential through the next elector's reign and passed down to Sybilla's husband, John.

The same year as her sister married, Anne's betrothal to the younger Francis, heir to the Duchy of Lorraine, was being negotiated. The Duke of Guelders from a neighbouring duchy had no heirs but many claimants to his lands. Anne's father, John III, was one of them and it was agreed that he would pass his claim on to his daughter and Francis of Lorraine (son of the duke's nephew) would become the duke's heir. The marriage contract was signed 5 June 1527 but there was no betrothal ceremony and Anne and Francis did not even meet nor give consent to the match. Francis was only nine at the time and beneath the age of consent so the contract was *de futura* – a promise to marry at a future date that was only legally binding if consummated. Anne would remain with her mother until she was in her twenties but this marriage contract would be called into question at a later date.

An alliance with England was considered at the Tudor court as early as May 1530 when Sir Herman Ryngk urged Henry VIII to consider an agreement with the Duke of Cleves in case of war with France, Burgundy or Spain as he possessed 'three most powerful duchies and two earldoms, and many towns not only strong but populous. If England were in danger he could alone raise an army sufficient to defend it; and he is descended from the same stock as the kings of England, as will be shown by a genealogy'.[4] Although not specifically stated the negotiations must have included a marriage with William 'fifteen years old, of middle height, brown complexion, sound in body and limbs well learned, and speaks Latin and French'[5] to the Princess Mary as Ryngk discounts Sybilla as being married, Anne contracted and Amelia still in her minority. Ryngk lived in Cologne but was a Hanseatic merchant of the London Steelyard and paid to bring news to Henry's court. His suggestion was followed in 1531 by a visit from Cleves ambassadors to further a marriage proposal. It was just one of several proposals for Henry VIII's daughter that would come to nothing. Though it was raised again in 1538, Mary would not marry until 1554 and then to Philip II of Spain.

Whilst Anne followed the religion of her Catholic mother, her sister was becoming more involved in the Protestant Reformation. In 1531, the Schmalkaldic League was formed of eight Lutheran princes across eleven cities in reaction to Charles V's insistence they return to the Catholic Church and the proposed election of Ferdinand as King of the Romans and the emperor's heir. This defensive league was headed by Anne's brother-in-law John Frederick and Philip, Landgrave of Hesse and commanded a military force of 10,000 foot and 2000 cavalry to protect its members from attack by Charles V and his allies. Trying to gain support from England they sent ambassadors to Henry VIII but for the time being he had no wish to become embroiled in their quarrels. Henry had no love of Luther's teachings. His title 'defender of the faith' had come about from writing his *Defence of the Seven Sacraments* that lambasted Luther's ideas yet the league might be an ally should England's relationship with the Holy Roman Emperor worsen.

John Frederick became Duke of Saxony after his father's death in August 1532 and encouraged Luther to continue his writings. Anne's sister Sybilla was as committed to reform as her husband was and corresponded with several of the key reformers of the times. One Justus Menius dedicated his work *Oeconomia Christiana* to her, a book that expounded on the correct way to keep a Christian household.

Anne's mother Maria had a Catholic confessor Dom Joannes Justus Lanspergius, a prodigious writer. Amongst his works were two papers scorning Lutheran beliefs, which Maria may well have shared with her daughter. Anne must have wondered why her sister was so supportive of the controversial reformer with ideals so contrary to her mother's and father's beliefs.

Sybilla may have married the head of the Protestant league but her father John, who leant more towards the teachings of Erasmus, banned the writings of Luther as 'vain, wrong and heretical'.[6] Anne never seems to have swayed from her mother's religion. Sybilla would write to Anne all their lives but the girls were very different and on matters of religion they would never agree.

Although Lutheran Protestantism was popular across Germany, Cleves was not overtly protestant and the duke was more concerned with Catholic reform. Anne's father was known as 'the peaceful' or more derogatory 'the simple' for trying to find a middle ground. The Cleves family motto was *candida nostra fides* – our faith is spotless. Konrad von Heresbach, the humanist scholar, acted as councillor to Anne's father and later as tutor to her brother William. His advice shaped John's revised Church Ordinance of 1533 which was taken to Erasmus for approval and would later earn him a pension from the duke. 'All preaching was to be based on scripture and the early Fathers and to avoid polemics; the preachers should be educated and properly appointed priests'.[7] It was 'a completely Erasmian reform'.[8]

John also reformed court behaviour with various proclamations that would affect Anne's life. He insisted that his court was orderly with no 'spontaneous parties'[9] or excessive drinking. Is it any wonder that Anne would be completely unprepared for life in another country? We could argue that Anne's early years were dull but she may have been quite content to be the devoted daughter who never strayed far from her mother. She may well have enjoyed her simple pastimes but in 1536 she was twenty-one and past marriageable age. She was surely considering who her swan knight would be. This family legend told of how the Cleves family were descended from the swan-knight Lohengrin who came to the rescue of Elsa of Brabant held in a castle in Cleves.

It was the day on which Elsa was to be wedded to her tyrant. She had spent the night in tears and bitter lamentations, and now, weary and distraught, too hopeless even for tears, she looked out from the bars of her prison with dull, despairing eyes. Suddenly she heard the melodious strains and a moment later saw the approach of a swan-drawn boat, wherein lay a sleeping knight. Hope leapt within her, for she remembered the prophecy of an old nun, long since dead, that a sleeping knight would rescue her from grave peril. Directly he stepped ashore the youth made his way to the place of her confinement and, espying her face at the heavily barred window, knelt before her and begged that she would take him for her champion.

At that moment the blast of a trumpet was heard, followed by the voice of the herald as, for the last time, he challenged any knight to take up arms on behalf of Elsa of Brabant. Lohengrin boldly accepted the challenge, and Telramund, when the news reached him of the unexpected opposition, on the very day he had appointed for his wedding, was surprised and enraged beyond measure, yet he dared not refuse to do battle with the stranger knight, because of the Emperor's decree. So it was arranged that the combat should take place immediately. News of it reached the people of Cleves, and a great concourse gathered to witness the spectacle, all of them secretly in sympathy with the persecuted maiden, though these feelings were carefully concealed from the ruthless Telramund.[10]

Elsa's swan-knight would remain with her on the condition she never asked his true identity. But before long curiosity got the better of her and she asked him who he was. *"Oh, Elsa,"* he said sorrowfully, *"thou knowest not what thou hast done. Thy promise is broken, and to-day I must leave thee for ever"*.[11] And with that he blew a blast on his silver horn and the boat he had arrived on returned, pulled by two white swans, to take him away from his wife and sons.

The tale was one of Germanic Arthurian literature first written by Wolfram van Eschenbach in *Parzival*, an epic poem c.1210. As with tales of myth and folklore there are many different versions but a later story linked the legend more directly with Cleves when Beatrice the only daughter of Dietrich, the Duke of Cleves, saw a boat being pulled along by a white swan with a gold chain carrying the knight Helias towards her. He married her and became Duke of Cleves but as with the earlier legend she broke their bond by asking who is was. He left his children his sword, his horn, and his ring before he sailed away. These children would carry on the line of the swan-knight as dukes of Cleves.

Swans were an ever present theme in Anne's life. She had two white swans as her heraldic device and the Schwanenburg, or Swan Castle, was one of her childhood residences used by the family in the spring and summer. Here the impressive 180 foot Swan Tower topped by a golden swan weather vane gave a vantage point from which to look out across the town of Cleve and the countryside beyond. Knights in Cleves joined the Order of the Swan founded by Frederick II of Brandenburg in 1440 and wore a badge depicting a silver swan with a gold chain, symbolism which would later be added to the Cleves coat of arms.

By the end of 1536, the man who was to be Anne's knight had already had two wives; Katherine of Aragon and Anne Boleyn and was married to his third Jane Seymour. Katherine had died in January alone and heartsick from being divorced from the king. Anne had been beheaded in May on trumped-up charges of adultery. One day later Henry VIII became betrothed to Jane Seymour and married her on 30 May. Recent events had changed the king of England from the athletic, glorious specimen of his youth to the fuller, harsher man of middle age he had become. She did not know it yet but Anne would soon be thrown into his world and he would prove to be no swan-knight.

Anne of Cleves

Chapter Two

The Search for a Bride
1537–1539

Early in 1537 John Husee, an agent of Lord Lisle's, the governor of Calais, wrote that the king of England hardly went out as his ulcerated leg was so sore. In Tudor times to reach the age of forty was an accomplishment and Henry was now forty-five. Physically he had managed to survive without suffering much illness. He had had bouts of malaria and smallpox and occasionally suffered from constipation. Two jousting accidents had rendered him blows to the head and caused him recurring headaches. He was fastidious about the risk of ill health, moving his court away from areas affected by prevalent disease like the sweating sickness and bubonic plague. He had suffered from ulcers on his leg from 1527 and liked coming up with his own remedies including *The King's Own Grey Plaster*, a remedy to ease his pain and reduce inflammation. Its ingredients included roots and buds from plants, vinegar, rosewater, ivory flakes, powdered pearls and less savoury ingredients like earthworms, lead, chicken and calf fat.

Mentally the king had been going through one of the toughest times in his life from his divorce to his marriage with his second wife Anne Boleyn and her subsequent trial and execution in 1536. The pope had threatened to excommunicate him and although Henry had promised in 1534 he would not 'decline or vary from the congregation of Christ's church in any things concerning the very articles of the Catholic faith of Christendom',[1] his relationship with Rome would worsen and his people would rise up against him. The Pilgrimage of Grace in 1536 was a rebellion that arose in Lincolnshire and Yorkshire due to Henry's policy of dissolving the monasteries, his break with Rome and many other grievances including those against chief minister Thomas Cromwell's policies. Cromwell had worked in Thomas Wolsey's household and risen to become the cardinal's secretary. By the end of 1530 he had joined the Privy Council and Henry made him chief minister and the king's principal secretary officially at the end of 1534. He was instrumental in both the king's divorce from Katherine of Aragon and Anne Boleyn's downfall. Cromwell was Henrys go-to man of 'singular excellence of wit, joined with an industrious diligence of mind'[2] but he was unpopular with the people for his sweeping reformations.

The Pilgrimage of Grace was a well organised uprising that swelled to over 30,000 men and 'After the king's highness was informed of this newly arisen insurrection he, making no delay in so weighty a matter, caused with all speed the Dukes of Norfolk and Suffolk, the marquis of Exeter, the earl of Shrewsbury and others, accompanied by his mighty and royal army which was of great power and strength, immediately to set upon the rebels. But when these noble captains and counsellors approached the rebels and saw their number and how they were determined on battle, they worked with great prudence to pacify all without shedding blood'.[3] In fact Henry's army was no match for the rebels and Norfolk persuaded their leaders to accept peace terms with promises of change and redress. It was not to be forthcoming and in July 1537 many of the rebels were executed.

Henry VIII was now married to Jane Seymour, the humble and pious wife, who bore him his longed for heir on 12 October 1537 but triumph soon turned to sorrow when she died twelve days later of puerperal fever 'and none in the realme was it more heavelier taken then of the kynges Maiestie him self, whose death caused the kyng immediately to remove into Westminster wher he mourned and kept him selfe close and secret a great while...'[4] Whilst he shut himself away with only his fool Will Somers for company, his councillors immediately began the search for a new wife. There was no suitable match in England

and Cromwell first set about contacting his contemporaries in France to enquire on the availability of King Francis I's daughter Margaret or possibly Marie de Guise, a widowed duchess.

Henry knew at his age that he could not wait too long to remarry. As the Duke of Norfolk said 'by reason of which more children might be brought forth'.[5] Jane had given him one male heir but he was still young enough to father more and make sure the succession was secure. His councillors were in agreement. Not only was there a need to secure the Tudor line but now Henry was Europe's most eligible bachelor, his marriage with a foreign princess could strengthen England's alliances. It could also change Europe's political outlook which was currently a power play between Francis I of France and Charles V, the Holy Roman Emperor.

England had signed a defensive treaty with France in 1532 and in September 1533 the French king was godfather to Henry's daughter Elizabeth. Francis I had supported Henry's marriage to Anne Boleyn but their relationship would be a fractious one as was Henry's relationship with Charles V, his nephew, through his marriage to Katherine of Aragon. The Holy Roman Emperor would never forgive him for his treatment of his aunt and the potential for foreign hostilities hung heavy in the air.

Both of these kings were Catholic and uncertain of where Henry VIII's loyalties lay and his relationship to church reform. In 1536 Henry devised the Ten Articles which laid down the official position of the church in England. It discussed three sacraments – baptism, penance and the Eucharist – yet failed to mention the sacraments of confirmation, ordination, marriage and last rites. It was a middle ground between Catholicism and Protestantism by which Henry 'preserved his freedom to move in either direction'.[6]

As far back as 1533 when Henry first heard the pope was threatening to excommunicate him Cromwell had started to look to Germany for an alliance. The king's minister sent Christopher

Mont to find out more about the German princes especially those opposed to Rome and their attitude towards England. It would foreshadow years of negotiations with the possibility of Henry joining the Schmalkaldic League – a move that Cromwell welcomed to further church reformation but also to provide mutual defence. Something of import if Francis I and Charles V were to turn against him. Henry welcomed theological discussions but would not commit himself. Still it raised the possibility of a marriage outside of Francis' and Charles' control.

It was John Hutton, ambassador to Dowager Queen Mary of Hungary, regent of the Netherlands, who first suggested Anne of Cleves in December 1537 but she was one at the end of an unflattering list and his report was not favourable. He wrote from Brussels:

> There is in the court waiting upon the Queen the daughter of the lord of Breidroot, 14 years old and of goodly stature, virtuous, sad and womanly. Her mother, who is dead, was daughter to the cardinal of Luike's sister; and the Cardinal would give her a good dote (dowry). There is a widow of the late earl of Egmond, who repairs often to the Court. She is over 40, but does not look it. There is the duchess of Milan, who is reportedly a goodly personage and of excellent beauty. The duke of Cleves has a daughter, but there is no great praise either of her personage or her beauty.[7]

It was her sister Sybilla that was known for her beauty not Anne.

Margaretha Brederode was the first candidate he mentioned. The motherless child of Lord Reinoud III van Bredrode was probably too young to be considered seriously and she was also a dependant of one Cardinal Liege who was a contemporary of Reginald Pole's, Henry's old enemy. Frances van Luxembourg, widow of Jan van Egmond by contrast was probably deemed too old at forty. Henry wanted a wife who would bear him children and Frances, although being a mother, would have been seen as past childbearing age.

Christina of Denmark, Duchess of Milan, and Anne of Cleves were still possibilities although the German reformer Melanchthon thought Christina had almost married Anne's brother William. He wrote to a friend 'The Widow of Milan, daughter of Christian, the captive King of Denmark, was brought to Germany to wed the young Duke of Juliers. This is now changed, for Juliers becomes heir to Guelders, against the Emperor's will, and the girl is offered to the Englishman, whom the Spaniards, aiming at universal empire, would join to themselves against the Frenchmen and us. There is grave matter for your consideration'.[8] However Henry had become fixated with the idea of Marie de Guise as his next wife even though she was promised to his nephew James V of Scotland, the son of his elder sister Margaret. It was the French ambassador, Louis de Perreau, Sieur de Castillon, who had to inform him that she was unavailable. Marie came from the powerful Guise family descended from John II of France and had proved she was fertile with two sons from her previous marriage to Louis II d'Orléans, the Duke of Longueville, who had died in 1537. Henry was not to be put off so easily. Castillon reported weeks later that the king was still 'amorous of Madame de Longueville' and that 'if matters were not so far advanced that they could not be broken off, to deliver her to him'. Henry promised 'he would do twice as much for you (Francis) as the king of Scots would'.[9] If Henry could marry Marie it would cement his relationship with France.

Marie herself had mixed feelings about the match. She is reported to have said when hearing Henry's comment he was 'big in person, in need of a big wife', that 'although she was very tall, her neck was very small'.[10] For any woman the prospect of marrying the king of England was a scary one given his treatment of his first wife and the execution of his second. James V by contrast had lost his first wife to illness and was a young, strong, athletic man whereas Henry was over twenty years older and past his prime. Still the king of England would be a prestigious match and the Guise family would welcome such a powerful ally. Yet the king of Scotland maintained the 'auld alliance' with France – a treaty in place since 1295 – and had not been as fickle in his political dealings as Henry. Either way Marie would be leaving France and her surviving son behind and ultimately it was not her decision to make.

Peter Mewtas, a gentleman of the privy chamber, was sent twice, to Chateaudun Castle and Joinville, to visit Marie of Guise and obtain her portrait. He was also to find out whether regardless of any arrangement with James V the widowed duchess would consider Henry as her next husband. Marie, playing for time, said her father had consented to her marriage to the Scottish king, although she had not, but she could only wed whomever King Francis I decided on. A letter from her mother suggests she was willing to see her daughter married to Henry but a marriage contract with James had already been settled so 'that things will not be done so much for your advantage as I wished'.[11] The situation was out of their control and Francis I had promised Marie to James after his first wife, the king's daughter Madeleine, had died after their short marriage in July 1537. Marie would marry Henry's nephew in Scotland in May and the king of England would have to look elsewhere.

His ambassadors had not been lax in finding out who else was available and in March 1538 Hans Holbein and Philip Hoby were sent to Christina of Denmark, the widowed duchess of Milan, now living in Brussels with her aunt, Mary of Hungary, to paint the sixteen-year-old's portrait. Christina was the niece of Charles V and would make a significant political match. Hutton described her as 'competent of beauty, of favour excellent, soft of speech and very gentle in countenance'.[12] She sat for three hours for the portrait. But her guardian Mary was unimpressed with any notion of a marriage to the English king. When Henry married Jane Seymour she had commented 'It is to be hoped – if one can hope anything from such a man – that when he is tired of this wife he will find some better way of getting rid of her. Women, I think, would hardly be pleased if such customs became general, and with good reason; and although I have no wish to expose myself to similar risks, yet, as I belong to the feminine sex, I, too, will pray that God may preserve us from such perils'.[13] Yet she had been unable to stop Christina's marriage at the age of thirteen to Francesco Sforza, Duke of Milan, a man twenty-six years older than her. Mary herself had been married to King Louis II of Hungary and Bohemia in 1515 but lost her husband at the Battle of Mohács in 1526. She had not wanted to become regent of the Netherlands but her brother Charles V had insisted telling her 'I am only one and I can't be everywhere; and I must be where I ought to be and where I can, and often enough only where I can be and not where I would like to be; for one can't do more than one can do'[14] and with that statement she could hardly refuse. With it came the guardianship of her nieces Dorothea and Christina. After the death of her husband Christina returned to her aunt's household. Wolsey had proposed a marriage between Dorothea and Henry's illegitimate son, the Duke of Richmond but this was rejected and she would instead marry Frederick of the Palatinate in 1535. At least she had escaped Henry's clutches.

The king was still very excited about the possibility of a marriage with Christina. She was young and beautiful by all accounts but while he waited for her portrait to arrive his health was suffering. His ulcerated leg was so bad that he had to have it lanced. Although it improved the sore, it would never heal completely and Henry was rapidly gaining weight since he could no longer participate in the sports of his youth. It didn't stop him from thinking he was a much sought-after husband and now he enthusiastically began to look at other marriage possibilities. Who else might make a suitable bride?

In May the French ambassador Castillon contacted the French court for suggestions of who else could be put forward as potential matches for Henry. Mary de Guises' younger sister Louise 'as beautiful and graceful clever and well fitted to please and obey'[15] was suggested as was her other sister Renee. Marie of Vendome, the eldest daughter of Charles de Bourbon and Anne of Lorraine, daughter of Antoine the Good, were also mooted. By June Holbein and Hoby were travelling back to France to paint Louise de Guises' portrait. Henry was happy with her likeness but wanted to see his bride in person. He may have been making a political alliance with his fourth marriage but he wanted a good-looking wife as well.

Sir Francis Bryan, Henry's friend and diplomat, was serving in France and knowing the king wished to see his potential brides suggested the king come to Calais, an English-owned port since 1347, where he could meet them. Henry certainly thought it a good idea writing to his ambassador at the imperial court:

His Grace prudently considering how that marriage is a bargain of such nature as may endure for the whole life of a man, and a thing whereof the pleasure and quiet, or the displeasure and torment of the man's mind doth much depend, thinketh it to be much necessary both for himself and the party with whom it shall please God to join him in marriage, that the one might see the other before the time they should be so affianced, as they might not without dishonour or further inconvenience break off.[16]

Bryan thought that Marguerite of Navarre, Francis I's sister, could chaperone a bevy of beauties from which the king could take his pick. Henry's desire for a French alliance was cooling due to King Francis signing the Truce of Nice with the Holy Roman Emperor in June, a ten year truce between these two powerful men that made no mention of England. In August Castillon urged his master to allow the meeting to go ahead but Francis refused. Henry told the ambassador 'By God, I trust no one but myself. The thing touches me too near. I wish to see them and know them some time before deciding'[17] but Francis was not happy at having his noble ladies trotted out for the English king's pleasure and his ambassador was told to put him off. This he did by ridiculing the situation and asking the king did he mean to sleep with them to test them out, which embarrassed Henry so much he gave up on the idea. He could still pursue Christina of Denmark after all even though her guardian had also refused a meeting in Calais. Negotiations had started and Charles V gave the unwilling Mary of Hungary permission to arrange their marriage.

Throughout the summer other possibilities were still being raised. Marriage negotiations could drag on and Henry continued to keep his options open. Cromwell, a key instigator of church reform, invited a delegation of German ambassadors to England to discuss further Henry's alliance with the Schmalkaldic League. By the time the embassy arrived in 1538 church reformation in England was in its infancy but Henry would not go the whole way and agree to the Confession of Augsburg, the twenty-eight articles of faith of the Lutheran church, as the League requested. While Cromwell continued to work towards an alliance with the Schmalkaldic League there was another way in which England could ally with Germany.

Franz Burchart, one of the delegates and also vice-chancellor of Saxony, thought the king might well marry a German princess and wrote to John Frederick, Anne of Cleves' brother-in-law and head of the league, that 'lord Cromwell, who is most favourably inclined to the German nation, wants most dearly that the king should wed himself with the German princes'.[18] It was also suggested again that the Princess Mary could marry William of Cleves.

Anne's brother William had become Duke of Guelderland giving the region more strategic importance and annoying Charles V who saw William and Cleves as a thorn bordering his Hapsburg lands in the Low Countries. The Holy Roman Emperor wrote how 'after the death of Charles of Egmont, Duke William of Cleves seized upon the government of the duchy of Guelders, asserting a claim to it. His Imperial Majesty, seeing how matters stood, and how he consequently ought to and could act, made him offers, the conditions of which were such that they ought reasonably to be accepted'[19] but William was not about to give up his hold on the area. It also had implications for his sister's betrothal to Francis of Lorraine, heir to Guelderland through their marriage treaty and the agreement between Anne's father and the previous duke. Francis could not be permitted to marry her now or William's new prize would be forfeit. Anne of Cleves was still available.

Cromwell was still hoping for a Cleves match but there were other candidates. In August Holbein and Hoby were sent to obtain a portrait of Marie de Guises' sister Renee to no avail as she was no longer in the marriage market after becoming a nun at St Peter's in Rheims. Louise was at home but ill. Her mother was wary of the ambassadors and wrote to her daughter Marie now married to James V in Scotland 'The gentleman (Hoby) came to see me, pretending that he was on his way to find the Emperor, and, having heard that Louise was ill, would not pass by without inquiring after her, that he might take back news of her health to the King his master. He begged to be allowed to see her, which he did, although it was a day when the fever was on her... He then told me that, as he was so near Lorraine, he meant to go on to Nancy to see the country. I have no doubt that he was going there to draw Mademoiselle's portrait, in the same way he has drawn others...'[20]

They did indeed travel on to Nancy to paint Anne of Lorraine, another possible bride. Later in the year, ambassadors were sent to pay court to Christina of Denmark to try and further marriage negotiations with the widowed duchess. Christina was extremely forthright in letting them know she hardly saw Henry as a suitable husband and 'that the King's Majesty was in so little space rid of the queens that she dare not trust his Council, though she durst trust his Majesty; for her council suspecteth that her great-aunt was poisoned, that the second was innocently put to death, and the third lost for lack of keeping in her childbed'[21] She certainly told it how it was although a comment attributed to her – that if she had two heads, she would give Henry one – was probably untrue. As she told Thomas Wriotheseley, she was at the Holy Roman Emperor's command to which he replied:

> Then I hope to be among the Englishmen that shall be first acquainted with my new mistress, for the Emperor hath instantly desired it. Oh, Madam, how happy shall you be if it be your chance to be matched with my master! You shall be matched with the most gentle gentleman that liveth, his nature so benign and pleasant that I think to this day no man hath heard many angry words pass his mouth. As God shall help me, if he were no King, instead one of the most puissant Princes of Christendom, I think, if you saw him, you would say that for his virtues, gentleness, wisdom, experience, goodliness of person, and all other gifts and qualities, he were worthy to be made a King. I know your Grace to be of goodly parentage, and to have many great Princesses in your family, but if God sent this to a good conclusion, you shall be of all the rest the most happy.[22]

Wriotheseley certainly knew how to talk favourably of the king even if no one believed his words. But Charles V was fast becoming annoyed at Henry's demands. Although a marriage treaty was being negotiated it frequently stalled. The English king wanted Christina rather than her older sister to succeed the Danish throne and revenues from the duchy of Milan he wanted protected in the event of French interference. At the same time negotiations for the Princess Mary to marry Dom Luis of Portugal, related to Charles V, rather than William of Cleves were running more smoothly but in the end would fail as would the negotiations for Henry's marriage to Christina of Denmark.

A papal dispensation was needed due to Christina's relationship to Katherine of Aragon and given Henry's current situation that would hardly be forthcoming. He had been excommunicated in December 1538 with Pope Paul III issuing a 'Bull against Hen. VIII., renewing the execution of the bull of 30 Aug. 1535, which had been suspended in hope of his amendment, as he has since gone to still further excesses, having dug up and burned the bones of St Thomas of Canterbury and scattered the ashes to the winds, (after calling the saint to judgment, condemning him as contumacious, and proclaiming him a traitor), and spoiled his shrine. He has also spoiled St. Augustine's monastery in the same city, driven out the monks and put in deer in their place'.[23] Henry's transgression included not only these points but his divorce, his dissolution of the monasteries, religious persecution and calling himself Supreme Head of the Church of England. The pope urged Francis I, Charles V and James V of Scotland to declare war on the heretic English king and the new year saw England in a frenzy of preparation should war be declared and an invasion attempted. Coastal fortifications were improved using stone from dissolved monasteries and beacons were made ready to signal an attack. Henry increased the ships in his navy and had his troops mustered should they need to set sail at a moment's notice. Likewise the Scottish border was reinforced and across the country men were made aware that they may be called to fight. Defences in Calais and Guisnes were also tightened. Henry rode out to Portsmouth to inspect his ships and check England's south coast defences.

The new French ambassador who replaced Castillon was Charles de Marillac. He informed Montmorency, Constable of France and Francis I's advisor:

The English continue to fortify the frontiers in all haste, and take musters everywhere, for which business the princes [sic] and other lords who have charge from the King are dispersed in different places. Cromwell returned the day before yesterday from a place 25 miles from hence where he had made a muster of 10,000 men, and next Friday, St. George's Day, that of London shall be made, which may be 50,000 or 60,000 men, for no one who can bear arms is excepted; even strangers here engaged in commerce are compelled to provide themselves harness and wear the livery of the city. Five or six ships do nothing but circle round the kingdom in order to explore and correspond if need be by fires with those who watch by night upon certain "gardes" of wood lately erected; so that no foreign vessel could show itself without the whole country being warned. Most of the King's ships of war have already made sail, and very few remain even of those taken from the King's subjects and strangers which are not in fighting order. Computes that the utmost number they can put to sea is 30 ships of 300 tons; 30 or 40 of 200, to 300 tons, and 80 of smaller burden. This may exceed the 150 sail that I wrote they intended to make, but for the present they have not more than 90 or 92 well equipped. Thinks if they can make 120 for this year it will be the utmost; and even that is much for the little time since they began.[24]

Henry was covering all his bases. As well as his country's preparation for war, he had sent Christopher Mont back to Saxony to talk with Anne's brother-in-law and members of the Schmalkaldic League about furthering their alliance. The king was not ready to join a Protestant League nor can we imagine he wanted to agree to the Confession of Augsburg but he did want allies. The League had a defensive force he could call on and so he asked that an embassy be sent to him to agree a common confession of faith.

Henry's marriage prospects lessened. Queen Mary of Hungary had no real desire to see Christina of Denmark married to the English king anyway and wrote to Charles V in January 1539:

If the King of England would seriously mend his ways and proceed to conclude the marriage in earnest, not merely to sow dissension between His Majesty and the King of France, this would no doubt be the most honourable alliance for the Duchess and the most advantageous for the Low Countries; but there is no evidence of this – rather the reverse, as your Ambassador in France tells us, from what he hears of the conversations held by King Henry with the French envoy in London. The Queen considers this point to be entirely settled, and it remains only to know Your Majesty's wishes. Are we to dissemble with the English as we have done till now, which, however, is very difficult, or are we to break off negotiations altogether? This can best be done by putting forward quite reasonable terms, but which are not agreeable to the King. The Queen begs His Majesty to tell her exactly what she is to do, remembering that the King of England, when he cannot ally himself with the Emperor or in France, may seek an alliance with Cleves, and will be further alienated from religion, and may do much harm by putting himself at the head of the German princes – all of which she prays Your Majesty to consider.[25]

Mary received no reply and in desperation wrote again 'I implore you tell me if I am to allow these conferences to drag on, for it is impossible to do this any longer without the most shameless dissimulation'.[26] Henry's ambassador Thomas Wriothesley, months later was still being entertained at her court, passing on messages from the king but never receiving a firm answer. Henry asked him to impress upon Mary of Hungary that 'old age was fast creeping on, and time was slipping and flying marvellously away'.[27] Wriotheseley tried a final time to get a definite answer asking her how Christina felt about the marriage given that 'divers malicious tongues, servants of the Bishop of Rome, had dared to speak lewdly in hugger-mugger of the King's Majesty'[28] and that he had heard Christina echoed their sentiments. Mary replied she had not heard Christina talking thus and 'that touching my niece's affection, I dare say unto you, that if the Emperor and your master the King agree upon this marriage, she will be at the Emperor's command'.[29] It still wasn't an answer.

Meanwhile Charles V and Francis I had signed the Treaty of Toledo agreeing that neither of them would treat with England without the other's consent. Finally Charles V declared that Henry's marriage to Christina could not take place without the pope's dispensation. Given Henry's excommunication that would not be forthcoming any time soon. The Archbishop of Canterbury could authorise the marriage in England but that would be unacceptable to Charles. Henry's break with the Holy Roman Church was complete and ambassadors were already on their way to Cleves.

Henry VIII

Chapter Three

Journey to England
1539

Henry VIII's deteriorating relationship with France and the Holy
Roman Empire meant that now an alliance with Germany was
much more appealing. John, Duke of Cleves, was not a Lutheran
nor a member of the Schmalkaldic League but he was open to
reform and remained independent and anti-papal. He could be
a useful ally should Francis I and Charles V carry out the Pope's
threat of war and he had two unmarried daughters, Anne and
Amelia.

When Henry sent Christopher Mont to John Frederick, the
Duke of Saxony, to discuss England joining the League, his
ambassador also had instructions to find out about the religious
inclination of the Duke of Cleves and his son, William. It is not
certain why he was to ask the Duke of Saxony rather than the
Duke of Cleves himself but Mont, always Cromwell's man, also
received instructions to:

*Diligently but secretly inquire of the beautie and qualities of the
lady eldest of booth doughters of the duke of Cleves, as well as what
shape, stature, proportion and complexion she is of as of her lerning
actyvitie, bihauiour and honest qualities...*[1]

If Mont heard that she 'as might be likened unto his Majesty'[2]
he was to further discussions on the marriage of Henry with the
eldest available daughter Anne and yet again the Princess Mary
with William, her brother. Chapuys, the Spanish ambassador,
reported to Charles V 'the French ambassador told me two
days ago that he had good authority for saying, though he was
sworn not to tell what authority, that this King was treating to

marry the Princess to the young Duke of Cleves, and thereby to league himself with the King of Denmark, the Dukes of Saxony and Prussia and the Landgrave of Hesse, offering a great sum of money, if need were, to carry on war against your Majesty'.[3] Mont had instructions to deal with Burchart, the Duke of Saxony's vice-chancellor and if he wished to see the princess' picture he 'shall remind him that she is a King's daughter and that it was never seen that the pictures of persons of such degree were sent abroad. Burgartus, too, has seen her and can testify of her proportion, countenance, and beauty, and though she is only the King's natural daughter she is endued, as all the world knows, with such beauty, learning, and virtues, that when the rest is agreed, no man would stick for any part concerning her beauty and goodness'.[4] Although Henry refused to send a picture of his daughter to her prospective husband, the king could not agree to his own marriage without seeing Anne's picture first. Mont was instructed to arrange for a portrait to be sent to England but at this time the court painter for Cleves, Lucas Cranach the elder, was unwell and unable to take up the commission.

There was a delay in further proceedings when Anne's father died at the beginning of February, making her twenty-three-year-old brother William his successor. In March Henry decided to send Edward Carne, Nicholas Wotton and Richard Beard to find out if the new duke was amenable to his sister's marriage to the king of England and also to 'have a sight of his eldest sister'.[5] That was easier said than done as when they did catch a glimpse of Anne and Amelia they were well covered but for 'a part of their faces, and that under such monstrous habit and apparel, was no sight, neither of their faces nor of their person'.[6] When the ambassadors complained to Olisleger, vice-chancellor to the Duke of Cleves, he responded 'What? Would you see them naked?'[7] There were portraits available by Barthel de Bruyn, a talented painter from Cologne, but as they could not verify their likeness it was decided to send Hans Holbein to give a true representation of the two sisters. Meanwhile reports were reaching Henry that Anne was 'as well for the face, as for the whole body, above all other ladies excellent. She as far excelleth the Duchess of Saxony as the golden sun excelleth the silver moon. Every man praiseth the good virtues and honesty with shamefacedness which plainly appeareth in the gravity of her countenance'.[8] But how could they have known if no one could see her? Cromwell who passed on the reports to his king made sure they were favourable but the king would take no one's word for it. He wanted to see her likeness and soon.

Meanwhile the ambassadors were waiting for a meeting with William, Duke of Cleves. He had been severely ill in March and his vice-chancellor continued to put them off until May when he confessed that William wished to confer with his brother-in-law John Frederick about the proposed marriage and he also had concerns about the issue of a dowry. Although the ambassadors would not find out until later it was Anne's previous betrothal to the Duke of Lorraine that William really wanted to discuss with the Duke of Saxony. Wotton and Beard reported to Cromwell:

And as for the lady Anne, he sayde, as to his frendis secretelye, that the old Duke of Cleves and the Duke of Lorayne hadde ben yn communicacion togither for the mariaige of the Marquyse, the duke of Loraynes sonne, and the said ladye Anne, and that they haddo gone so ferre that wrytinges wer made and sealyd up on hit, and that the duke of Cleves hadde payed therupon to the duke of Gheldres by the said agreement certeyn sommes of money, and hadde fulfilled on his part all thinges, saving that the lady Anne was not yet maryed to the said Marquyse. Why then, quod we, it is but yn vayne to speake enye more of my ladye Anne, for she is fast ynnough ensueryd all redye. Naye, quod the Chawncelour, not so, for these promyses wer made onelye betwixte the fathers, and the partyes as yet have not gyven theyr consentes, but ar at theyr libertye to do what they wille.[9]

Content that Anne was free to marry, the ambassadors continued their negotiations but in the midst of their discussions Henry published his Act of Six Articles, a further statement of belief in the church in England that showed distinct Catholic leanings. Protestants termed it the 'bloody whip with six strings'[10] and saw it as a blow to the reform they had all hoped for. Where once John Frederick of Saxony had supported Henry's marriage into Cleves, this act now showed him that the king of England would never fully embrace the Convention of Augsburg and join the League and so his support wavered. His opinion, although William had sought it, did not deter Anne's brother. He still had yet to make a decision on his sister's fate. Frustrated, the English ambassadors waited impatiently. They had hoped to be returning to England with the marriage arranged by now.

With no definitive answers by July, Dr William Petre was sent to specifically have an audience with Maria of Julich-Berg, Anne's mother, to see if she was favourable to her daughter's marriage as well as to view any documents relating to Anne's pre-contract to the Duke of Lorraine. It seems that Amelia, Anne's younger sister, may have still been in the running at this stage as Petre had instructions on how to dissemble should she be offered:

If the lady Anne is promised past retraction but that the younger daughter is free, they shall answer that the King conceived from the Chancellor's words "that the m[arriage of] the lady Anne was not so far past but that [the King] might have had his election of both the daughters [to have] chosen her, that for her age had been most meet f[or him]," and therefore before writing the said reply to the King they would like to see the said [pacts] to learn "whether anything hath bee[n] ... sithens the time of the making thereof that mig[ht be] any further impediment." They shall press them on this; but if they persist in the overture of the youngest daughter, Wotton and Peter shall, as of themselves, say merrily that they think all should be one to the King, but as his Grace preferred the eldest they must refer again to him.[11]

On 11 August Wotton sent back a report confirming again that Anne was not bound by any covenants made by the old Duke of Cleves and the Duke of Lorraine and he furnished Henry with more details about his potential bride. He confirmed her sheltered upbringing and closeness to her mother. She spent most of her time at her needlework, couldn't read or write French or Latin, nor sing or play an instrument. She only spoke German but her wit was good and Wotton had no doubt she would learn English when she put her mind to it. She was also not a drinker. It was a mixed report. Since Anne's mother had never expected her to marry a foreign king, her upbringing had been entirely suitable for a noble lady. Henry's first wife Katherine of Aragon hadn't spoken English either when she first arrived in England to marry his brother Arthur although she did know Latin and of course Spanish. Marillac, the French ambassador, reported 'The King, who in some former years has been solitary and pensive, now gives himself up to amusement. He evidently delights now in painting and embroidery'[12] so they had that in common! Henry also wouldn't want a drunkard for a wife so there was nothing in Wotton's report that deterred him.

Wotton finished by stating that Holbein 'hath taken the effigies of my Lady Anne and the Lady Amelia and hath expressed their images very lively'.[13] Holbein had taken a week to sketch both the sisters at the Palace of Duren which earnt him £40 from the king for his expenses. He was back at court at the beginning of September. The French ambassador Marillac confirmed his arrival and that shortly after a courier came with secret news for the king. The court was awash with rumour that Henry would marry soon.

Holbein had turned his sketches into 'tempera on parchment, which he glued on to canvas when he reached London'.[14] Anne's portrait was shown first to the king's chief minister. 'When

Cromwell saw the portrait, and found the lady was pretty, he was very glad'.[15] He waited until he was sure that Henry was in a good mood before showing it to him. We do not know the king's reaction to Holbein's work but it cannot have been unfavourable at the time.

Holbein had chosen to paint Anne square-on which was not typical of his usual studies. It has led some writers to postulate that he spent more time enriching her dress and jewels with rich regal colours of red, gold and green rather than concentrating on her face which can appear lifeless with dull eyes and only a faint suggestion of a smile. There have even been suggestions of hidden imagery that Holbein included as a warning to the king that perhaps Anne was not the bride for him. X-rays under the top layer of paint have shown that Holbein did alter her nose to make it shorter but like any artist's work adjustments would be made until they were happy with the final product. Holbein was known for painting good likenesses – Wotton certainly thought it was – and since the marriage negotiations continued Henry must have been happy to proceed.

With confirmation his intended was indeed free, Henry would marry Anne of Cleves. Henry would later tell Marillac he was marrying Anne to ally with Germany, that Cleves could provide 'a diversionary military action'[16] if England was attacked and ultimately because she was of child-bearing age. William of Cleves signed an initial marriage treaty on 4th September 1539 at Dusseldorf. Anne was present to thank the people of Cleves and her brother 'for having preferred her to such a marriage that she could wish for no better'.[17] Two days later the Duke of Cleves sent his ambassadors headed by Olisleger and Burchart to England to negotiate the finer points of the treaty, the dowry and income.

But Marillac was reporting that this might not yet come to pass. Duke Frederic, the brother of Louis V, prince elector of the Palatinate had arrived in England.

Probably duke Frederic, who appears a true servant of the Emperor, will try to break off this alliance with Cleves, in order that the duke of Cleves may not strengthen himself with English money to resist the Emperor's designs against him, through Gueldres, where he has proceeded so far, and will put forward urgently the marriage of the duchess of Milan. The whole to get money if possible; but such is the nature of this nation that he will get no pecuniary assistance except by compulsion.[18]

Frederick was married to Christina of Denmark's sister Dorothea and it seems as if he was trying to raise funds to free the girls' father, Christian II of Denmark, who had been imprisoned since 1531. He may have been trying to use Christina as a bargaining tool but Henry was past that now. Their marriage had already proved unfeasible and the Cleves negotiations were advancing quickly. Frederick's attempt to raise support for the Danish king was unsuccessful and Dorothea would later write to Anne to use her influence with Henry VIII to affect her father's release from prison.

The Cleves ambassadors arrived in London on 18 September and were escorted to Windsor where they spent the next eight days being royally entertained by Henry before settling the marriage negotiations. Henry tasked Cromwell, Cranmer, Lord Audley, Suffolk, Southampton and Tunstall, Bishop of Durham, to act on his behalf. It was agreed that the Duke of Cleves would provide a dowry of 100,000 gold florins, 40,000 to be paid on their wedding day and the rest within the year. Her dower payment was agreed at '20,000 golden florins of the Rhine, equal to 5,000 mks sterling money of England, as long as she remains in England'[19] after the death of the king. If she were to be childless and return home, her pension would be 15,000 florins, payable half-yearly for life, and she could keep her own dresses and jewels. They also agreed her inheritance rights with regards to Cleves. William was to pay for her travel to Calais within two months from where Henry would arrange and pay for her journey across the Channel. If safe conduct could not be guaranteed through Charles V's dominions, William would have to pay for the costs of her travel from another seaport. The marriage treaty was finalised on 24 September and the Cleves ambassador hastened back to William where at the beginning of October it was ratified. Meanwhile Henry waivered the dowry payment, knowing William could not afford it. It had been included in the treaty to save William's honour. Henry never expected riches from Cleves – just his bride.

Cromwell would have his work cut out for him over the following months as he looked to who should form the queen's household. To begin with he sent Mrs Gilman with four servants to Anne in Cleves perhaps to begin teaching her English and acquaint her with the country she would soon reside in. Susanna Gilman was the daughter of Gheraert Horenbout of Ghent and sister to the court painter Lucas Horenbout and a skilful illuminator and miniature painter herself. She had served in Jane Seymour's household and was now given £40 to travel to Germany to meet her new mistress.

A decision had to be made on how exactly Anne would travel to England. There were two routes; the first overland to Calais and then across the Channel, the other to sail from Harderwijk on the Zuiderzee. For Anne to travel overland permission had to be sought for safe conduct through the emperor's territories and he was still currently at odds with Anne's brother over Guelderland.

Henry thought it would be better for her to sail from the Cleves-owned port. He sent John Aborough of Devon and Richard Couche of Dover, experienced seamen, to investigate the route and draw up a 'rutter' – a mariner's guide to navigation and the first of its kind – and a rough chart. Henry was 'marvellously inflamed, supposing many things to be done thereon'[20] on seeing the rough sketch. In the finished drawing it showed Henry's flagship waiting at sea with a blockade of English ships to ensure Anne was safely escorted aboard. It would be a chance for Henry to show off how truly impressive his fleet was but the rutter also showed how dangerous the journey could be 'the deepest water that is betwixt Harddyerwek and Ankcewson is 3 fathoms (or) 19 foot water and in the channel is ooze... when you be nearer the coast you shall have sand, but no good ship may come so near'.[21]

However the Cleves envoys were concerned for Anne's health should she have to take such a long and dangerous sea journey. They worried she would 'take such cold or other disease, considering she was never before upon the seas, as should be to her great peril and the King's Majesty's great displeasure' and that also they feared 'how it might alter her complexion'.[22] They insisted she travel by land to Calais and thankfully Charles V gave her safe conduct through the Netherlands even though the pope wrote to him and Francis I to deny her passage 'if it is true she is a Lutheran'.[23] She wasn't and this must have been proved. At the end of October Henry wrote to Mary of Hungary that he was grateful for Charles' consent and that she 'may be pleased, for the personal security and comfort of the said lady (Anne) and suite, to add to her passport such full orders and favourable commendations as may be required and it is in your power to give since such is, as We can see, the good intention of our said brother, the Emperor'.[24] Mary would have no problem with Anne's journey through the Netherlands. She was probably still relieved that at least the English king was not marrying her niece.

Henry was anxious to receive his new bride but Anne had preparations to make with her mother including the making of a new wardrobe. Although her brother had few funds, she could not become a queen without the most regal clothing. Her brother William had to arrange her escort, plan her route and send ambassadors ahead to inform the heads of the relevant towns where accommodation needed to be organised. By the end of November Henry had expected Anne's arrival. He impatiently sent a courier to Cleves to find out what was going on as he was hoping for a Christmas wedding. He was assured that she would be in Calais on 8 December.

Anne left Dusseldorf on 26 November for the Schwanenburg or Swan Castle in Cleves where she was to meet her entourage. William had sent out a decree at the beginning of November for all the men to accompany her to meet there appropriately attired and with armour on the 25th. None of her family were to travel with her as they were still in mourning for her father and here she had to say goodbye to the mother she had always been close to, her sister Amelia (who would never marry) and her brother William.

With 263 attendants and 228 horses she set off on a journey that was as slow as five miles a day. No wonder given the amount of people not to mention the baggage that slowly wound its way through the Low Countries. Wotton's report to Cromwell details the array of people that would accompany her:

It is purposed to send over the following persons with Lady Anne, to continue with her, Mistress Gylmyn, who is taken for first of her gentlewomen, because she was sent here by the King, and four servants; also the widow of the late lord of Wissem, sister to Willik, steward of Cleves, who is "howmestrinne," i.e., governor to the other gentlewomen, with five servants; five other young gentlewomen, one being a baron's daughter called Swartzenbroch, with three to wait on them; eight pages, one being son to the earl of Waldeck, my lady's cousin germain, an aged gentleman, named Tennagel, my lady's steward, formerly the Duke's waltgrave, i.e. master of forests, with six persons, eight young gentlemen, four with two servants, and four with one. There are also a secretary, a chaplain and others. Making in all 88 persons. The following will come over with her but return: — The ambassadors of Saxe, the

Marshal Dultzik, and the vice-chancellor Burgartus, the earl of Oversteyn, the steward Hoghesteyn, and Dr. Olisleger with their servants. The following will come to Calais, but not cross unless the King desires it:—The young earl of Nuenare, whose wife is a kinswoman of my lady, and would have come but that she fell sick. He speaks Latin and French well besides his own tongue. With him is a gentleman named Roussenberg. Also the elder Palant, lord of Bredebent, one of the Duke's Council, John Buren, drossart or captain of Tolhuis, Hantzeler, drossart of Millen, the younger Palant, a knight of the Sepulchre (the elder Palant of Bredebent, and he be brothers and jolly fellows both), and 26 other gentlemen. There are also 13 trumpeters sent by the elector of Saxony and other officers and servants. The lady Keteler and the elder Palant's wife are also going.[25]

Anne travelled in a chariot of 'well carved gilt with arms of her country curiously wrought and covered with cloth of gold'.[26] Her first main stop was at Antwerp where Cromwell had arranged her reception. Antwerp was the capital of the Low Countries and a trade centre popular with the English. Here crowds gathered to see the new queen of England and Wotton reported it was a 'goodly sight'.[27] She was greeted by fifty English wool merchants from the Company of Merchant Adventurers dressed in velvet coats adorned with gold chains who escorted her by torchlight, even though it was day, to the English house on Old Bourse Street, their headquarters, for entertainment and refreshment. Stephen Vaughan, a contemporary of Cromwell's and head of the company was responsible for Anne's care whilst Lord Buren ensured all her attendants were well looked after.

The next day she continued her journey with some of the English merchants accompanying her as far as Stekene. After taking their leave the procession moved onwards to Bruges but was delayed due to the horses not being able to cross the River Schelde at low water. On she travelled through Dambrugh and

Newport. At Dunkirk she heard a sermon that was deemed to be heretic by some and prompted Henry to order an investigation but it was deemed not to be of 'any danger or hazzard'.[28]

Whilst Anne progressed slowly through town and country, Henry was ordering preparations to be made for her arrival. Only Thomas Cranmer, Archbishop of Canterbury had any misgivings at this stage. Although he was also an ardent believer in church reform and supported efforts to join the Schmalkaldic League, he felt that Henry should marry 'where that he had his fantasy and love, for that would be most comfort for his grace' rather than making a political match but Cromwell was adamant there was no suitable English bride and Cleves was an advantageous match to which Cranmer replied 'it would be very strange to be married with her that he could not talk withal'.[29]

Back in October Cromwell wrote to Lord Lisle, governor of Calais to improve the town especially the Exchequer House.

The king's Majesty's pleasure is that you shall view his Grace's house here called the Exchequer, that with all diligence all things therein necessary to be amended may be undelayedly repaired... Furthermore, his Majesty would that you should cause the streets and lanes there to be viewed for the pavements, and where any default is, to give commandment to those which should repair the same to see it immediately amended, endeavouring yourselves to put all other things within the said town in the most honest and cleanly order you can devise...[30]

Although Anne wasn't specifically mentioned it was obvious that Calais was to host someone of great import and Lord Lisle had heard rumours of marriage negotiations. Calais was in need of much repair and the 'other things' included renovating the Lantern Gate, the main entrance to the town, tidying the tiltyard, repairing walls and cleaning the entire town before even the work of decoration, fresh paint and royal emblems could be undertaken.

The men that were needed for the improvements included '9 free masons, 4 sawyers, a carpenter's apprentice, 14 bricklayers out of England, 15 of the town and marches, 10 bricklayers' prentices, 18 labourers making mortar, 9 water bearers, 85 mortar bearers, 50 bearers of chalk to the bricklayers, 29 labourers digging in the foundation, &c., 30 boys bearing of brick and chalk, 15 labourers burning of lime and hewing of chalk at Bullen Well, 6 slakers of lime, 3 water-bearers to them, 4 labourers lading cartes at the brickery, 5 working in the Braies at 9¾d., 5 cutting turfs at 8d., 8 casting earth behind the turfs, 2 watchers, 8 daily labourers, 4 labourers appointed by the King's bill, and 4 clerks'.[31] Calais was thrown into a frenzy of activity to make Calais, the first English town Anne would see, anywhere near presentable.

Lodgings also had to be prepared for her onward route once she arrived on English soil at Deal, Dover, Canterbury, Sittingbourne, Dartford and Greenwich. The roads she would travel down had to be clean and free of obstruction. Royal beds were sent to Dartford and Rochester and the Queens Apartments at Hampton Court Palace were redecorated. Cromwell has his work cut out for him sending orders out across the country and over the Channel. Amongst his duties was the organisation of Anne's new household.

Thomas Manner, Earl of Rutland, who had previously served Jane Seymour was appointed as her chamberlain, Sir Edward Baynton who had served both Jane Seymour and Anne Boleyn was made her vice-chamberlain, and John Dudley her master of horse. Six ladies-in-waiting were employed – Lady Margaret Douglas, the king's niece, the Countess of Sussex, the duchesses of Richmond and Suffolk, Lady Howard and Lady Clinton (formerly Bess Blount). Her maids of honour included Katherine Howard, Mary Norris, Anne Bassett (another young girl who had caught the king's eye) and Katherine Carey (later

Knollys), with the mother of maids Lady Browne to take charge of them all. Henry also reformed his Band of Spears. Headed by Sir Anthony Browne, fifty gentlemen pensioners would be an impressive guard to accompany the king and escort Henry to meet his new bride.

She reached Gravelines, just a few miles from Calais on 10 December, a little later than expected. Lord Lisle, governor of Calais, met Anne to escort her into the town the next day. She was greeted outside the town by the William Fizwilliam, Earl of Southampton and Lord Admiral, dressed in robes of cloth of gold and purple, 'who had in his companie thirtie gentlemen of the king's household, as Sir Francis Brian, Sir Thomas Seimer (Seymour), and others, beside a great number of gentlemen of his owne retinue clad in blue veluet, and crimson satin, and his yeomen in damaske of the same colours. The mariners of his ship were apparelled in satin of Bridges, cotes & slops of the same colour. The lord admerall brought her into Calis by lantern Gate. There was such a peale of ordinance shot off at his entrie, as was maruellous to the hearers'.[32] The king's ships the Lyon and the Sweepstake had fired 150 rounds of ammunition which created so much smoke the gathered nobles and Anne's entourage could hardly see one another. Lady Lisle was waiting with her ladies to escort Anne to the Exchequer, the king's lodging house. On the way 'The maior presented hir with an hundred markes in gold, the merchants of the staple with an hundred sovereigns of gold in a rich purse'.[33] One of the reception committee, Cromwell's son Gregory, assumed Anne would only be in Calais for two days and would sail that Sunday across the Channel as long as the weather was favourable. In fact it would be over two weeks until Anne could leave the English-owned port. Southampton was anxious for Henry's bride to be on her way and organised men to watch for signs of the weather changing. Anne agreed to be ready to leave at a moment's notice. She was as eager as he to embark on the next stage of her journey.

The next day Southampton took her on a tour of the harbour to show her Henry's fleet 'which were not only right well-appointed and trimmed with streamers, banners and flags, but also no less furnished with men standing in their tops, the shrouds, the yard-arms and other places'.[34] Anne was suitably impressed and overwhelmed as she was led from banquet to tournament. No expense was spared in her entertainment which had to be hastily arranged for her prolonged stay. Southampton was also impressed with Anne and reported 'the notable virtues of my lady now with her excellent beauty, such as I well perceive to be no less than was reported'.[35]

To pass the time over the coming days Anne asked Southampton to show her a card game that Henry liked to play. She wanted something to do to fill the anxious hours ahead and was worried she would have little in common with the king. 'And so my Lord William and I played with her at cent and Mr Morison, Mrs Gilmyn and Mr Wooton stood by and taught her to play. And I assure your Majesty she played as pleasantly and with as good a grace and countenance as ever in all my life I saw any noble woman'.[36]

Anne invited Southampton and other nobles to her apartments for an evening meal but the lord admiral was concerned at the king's reaction to such informality as with the playing of cards but Anne assured him otherwise and the admiral with the Lords Howard, Hastings, Talbot, Grey and Bryan, Knyvet, Seymour and Cromwell's son spent a pleasant evening with the bride-to-be. Anne was feeling a little homesick and a lot of apprehension as the days passed. When messages came from Flanders, she asked Southampton to see if there were any letters for her from home and was saddened when there were none. The longer she waited, the more alone she felt.

Lady Lisle did her best to make sure Anne was comfortable and had everything she needed. Her own daughter Anne had been selected for the queen's household in England and while

Lady Lisle hoped her other daughter Katherine may find a place in the new household she wrote to England with news from Calais. Anne replied 'I humbly thank your ladyship of the news you write me of her Grace, that she is so good and gentle to serve and please. It shall be no little rejoicement to us, her Grace's servants here, that shall attend daily upon her. And most comfort to the king's majesty, whose Highness is not a little desirous to have her Grace here'.[37]

Henry was growing more and more impatient by the day but finally the weather changed and Anne departed Calais for her new home and new husband on 27 December.

Princess Elizabeth

Chapter Four

The Marriage
1539–1540

Anne arrived at Deal on the east coast at 5 pm to be greeted by Sir Thomas Cheyne, Lord Warden of the Cinque Ports. She was escorted to the newly built Deal Castle, one of three new fortifications built to protect the Kent coast from invasion, to rest but as it was a small garrison fort, it was deemed more appropriate that she should spend the night at Dover Castle which had been sumptuously refurbished for her arrival. She was introduced to the Duke and Duchess of Suffolk, who would become her friend throughout her life, and Richard Sampson, the Bishop of Chichester, who were to escort her along the coast to more suitable accommodation. Exhausted from her whole day's voyage she was grateful to arrive at 11 pm and have the next day to rest before continuing her journey. Henry was waiting for news at Hampton Court, anxious that all should go well on his bride's journey up to London where they would officially meet for the first time.

The weather was foul on 29 December 1539 but Anne refused to be put off and once all her baggage and train was assembled, she set off for Canterbury. Charles Brandon, Duke of Suffolk, and Cheyne reported to Henry in the evening that even though wind and hail blew 'contynuelly in her face', Anne was 'desirous to make haste to the King ('s Highness) that her Grace forced for no nother, which (we) perceyvyng were very gladde to set her G(race) furthwards, considering if we should h(ave) lost this day'.[1]

Thomas Cranmer, Archbishop of Canterbury, met Anne halfway on the sixteen-mile journey to Canterbury at Barham Down. He had worried that the pouring rain would put off the gentlemen of the county. He detained one of Cromwell's servants to help rally attendees. 'In case he and other gentlemen of the country, with mine own retinue, had not the better assisted me, over and besides the number appointed, I should have received her Grace but with a slender company. For the whole number appointed to me, besides mine own company, was not six score, and yet some of them failed; so that if, partly by mine own company, and partly by other gentlemen's assistance; it had not been supplied, I should not have received her with a convenient number.'[2] But whether she noticed a smaller group or not, Anne was anxious to continue the journey and get out of the driving rain. After being presented with a cup full of gold coin, she was escorted to St Augustine's Abbey which had been refurbished and new queen's lodgings added especially for her visit. James Needham, Surveyor of the King's Works, had been in charge of '350 craftsmen and labourers on the site' who had worked through the nights using '31 dozen candles'.[3] As well two new ranges of chambers, Anne's arms were placed in the waiting chamber, two in her presence chamber and one over the stairs as well as the stained-glass windows carrying depictions of her badges alongside Henry's. All for just a one night stay.

Anne was gladdened by so much effort having been made on her behalf and even more so by the '40 or 50 gentlewomen (who waited) in velvet bonnets to see her, all which she took very joyously, and was so glad to see the King's subjects resorting so lovingly to her, that she forgot all the foul weather and was very merry at supper'.[4] The next night's accommodation was not as impressive being in Sittingbourne where an inn, possibly The Lion where Henry had stayed in 1532, had to be utilised but they soon travelled on to Rochester. The Duke of Norfolk, Lord Dacre, Lord Mountjoy and their men met her at Rainham Down and escorted her to the Bishop's Palace there.

Anne must have been overwhelmed by all the new places and people, especially as they were all talking to her in a language she did not know. None of the nobles had sent back any reports to Henry that depicted Anne in a harsh light but in Rochester she would meet Lord and Lady Browne who would supervise her maids. Lady Browne was appalled by what they saw. Perhaps knowing the king's taste Lady Browne despaired of the wedding to come and felt that 'the King should never heartily love her'.[5] Her husband was also troubled. When sent to Anne for the first time with a message from the king:

> *Having conceived in his mind, what was by picture and advertisements signified of her beauty and qualities, at the general view of the ladies he thought he saw no such thing there, and yet were thither of better favour than the queen. But when he was directed unto herself, and advisedly loked upon her, he saith, he was never more dismayed in all his life, lamenting in his hart, which altered his outward contenace, to se the lady so far and unlike that was reported, and of such sort as he thought the King's Highnes should not content himself with her. Nevertheles at his retorne to the Kings Majesty with her answer, the said Sir Anthony said nothing, ne nurst not.[6]*

Henry had grown impatient to see his intended. Burning with the ideal of chivalric love, so much a part of his youth, he rode down to Rochester on New Year's Day to see his wonderful new bride and 'nourish love'. Browne had not warned him nor had any one else mentioned Anne's appearance. They were obviously waiting for the king's reaction but many could see this young girl from Germany would not be to his liking. There are several accounts of their first meeting but Chapuys, the Spanish ambassador wrote:

> *And on New Year's day, in the afternoon, the king's grace with five of his privy chamber, being disguised with mottled cloaks with hoods so that they should not be recognised, came secretly to*

Rochester, and so went up into the chamber where the said lady
Anne was looking out of a window to see the bull-baiting which was
going on in the courtyard, and suddenly he embraced and kissed
her, and showed here (sic) a token which the King had sent her for
(a) New Year's gift, and she being abashed and not knowing who it
was thanked him, and so he spoke with her. But she regarded him
little, but always looked out the window... and when the King saw
that she took so little notice of his coming he went into another
chamber and took off his cloak and came in again in a coat of purple
velvet. And when the lords and knights saw his grace they did him
reverence... and then her grace humbled herself lowly to the king's
majesty, and his grace saluted her gain, and they talked together
lovingly, and afterwards he took her by the hand and led her to
another chamber where their graces amused themselves that night
and on Friday until the afternoon.[7]

Anne can hardly be blamed for not recognising the king. He was
just another courtier in a sea of unfamiliar faces that she had
seen since her arrival in England. Henry had expected her to see
him for who is was even in disguise as true love would always
know its mate. What happened next also has different versions.
Wriothesely echoed Chapuys when he wrote in his chronicle
that the king spoke lovingly to Anne and spent the evening with
her. Sir Anthony Browne however, echoing his wife's previous
assumption, had Henry practically running for the door. As
Starkey has pointed out Browne was one of Henry's closest men
and would have seen Henry's reaction and felt his displeasure
when the king was once more alone in his rooms. Wriothesely
only saw what was a public display.

Henry had seen Anne's portrait so seeing his bride in reality
should have been no shock. Holbein was known for his lifelike
paintings. Even if he had embellished her attributes the painting
must have shown a relatively good resemblance. Given what
was to follow, Holbein would have been the first to feel Henry's

wrath if the picture had been misleading. Admittedly Anne looked different in her German dress and spoke differently in her native tongue but what really irked Henry is that she had embarrassed him in front of his nobles. But for Henry to treat Anne in any other way than respectful would cause a diplomatic crisis. He left the next day to return to Greenwich and it is then that he began to talk of his displeasure with those closest to him. We know how he felt from the dispositions that would be later be given as evidence for the dissolution of his marriage. Henry then admitted '…when I saw her at Rochester, the first time I saw her, it rejoiced my heart that I had kept me free from making any pact or bond before with her till I saw her myself; for then I assure you I liked her so ill, and so far contrary to that she was praised, that I was woe she ever came into England'.[8]

At the time the king did not know what to do. He was so unhappy with what he had seen, he left before giving Anne her New Year's gift of sable furs telling Browne to give them to her and moaning 'I see nothing in this woman as men report of her, and I marvel that wise men would make would make such a report as they have done!'[9] The Earl of Southampton had been one of the last to send his comments on Anne to the king. Henry took him to task asking 'How like you this woman? Do you think her so fair and of such beauty as report hath been made unto me of her? I pray you tell me the truth'. The earl diplomatically answered that 'he took her not for fair, but to be of a brown complexion'.[10] Never once did Henry call her a Flanders mare. This would be suggested in Gilbert Burnet, Bishop of Salisbury's book, *The History of the Reformation of the Church of England*, written in 1679 that Henry 'swore they had brought over a Flanders mare to him; and was sorry it had gone so far, but glad it had proceeded no further' and echoed in Smollett's *History of England* not published until 1759.

Henry wanted answers from Cromwell. It was he who had arranged this marriage and Henry no longer wanted it to go ahead. Whilst Anne was moving from Rochester to Dartford, coming ever closer to London, Henry was demanding a remedy to the situation. Cromwell 'knew none'[11] and tried to blame the Earl of Southampton for bringing Anne to England knowing that Anne 'was not so handsome as had been represented'.[12] But the earl was furious and told them that he had done exactly as he had been ordered and that 'as the Princess was generally reported for a beauty, he had only repeated the opinions of others, for which no one ought reasonably to blame him, especially as he had supposed she would be his queen'.[13] Henry didn't blame him. He blamed Cromwell.

It was too late to do anything for now. Anne's formal reception at Greenwich was organised for the next day, 3 January. Proclamations had already declared 'that all who loved their lord the King should proceed to Greenwich to meet and make their devoir, to my Lady Anne of Cleves, who would shortly be their queen'.[14] Anne was escorted by the Dukes of Norfolk and Suffolk, the Archbishop of Canterbury and other nobles to Shooters Hill, near Blackheath where luxurious tents of cloth of gold had been prepared for her with scented braziers warming the air. Nothing as grand as the Field of the Cloth of Gold but still a magnificent display of Henry's wealth and a heartfelt welcome for the queen to be. She was greeted by the nobles of her new household, the Earl of Rutland and Sir Thomas Denny who presented her to the other officers that would serve her. Then

...doctor Daye appointed to her Almoner, made to her an eloquent oration in Latin, presenting to her on the kynges behalf all the officers and servauntes: which oracion was aunswered unto by the Duke her brothers Secretarie there being present, whiche done, the lady Margarete Doglas, daughter to the Quene of Scottes, the lady Marques Dorcet, daughter to the French Quene being nieces to the kyng, and the Duches of Rychemond, and the Countesse of Rutland and Herfford with divers other ladies and gentlewomen, to

the number of xv saluted and welcomed her grace, whiche alighted
out of her chariot in the which she had ridden all her long journey,
and with most goodly demeanour and loving countenaunce gave to
them hertie thankes and kissed them al, and after all her counsellors
and officers kissed her hand, which done, she with al the ladies
entered the tentes and there warmed them a space.[15]

Her brother's secretary who had travelled with her interpreted
their addresses and stood by her side until all the introductions
were finished. With great relief Anne took refreshment and
steeled herself for the next round of greetings and her meeting
with the king.

Henry was waiting just through the park at Greenwich for
word of Anne's arrival. The whole route was lined with merchants
from the Steelyard, aldermen and city officials, knights and
pensioners all wearing their finest clothes to witness the meeting
of Henry and Anne. Barriers had been erected along by the river
so that no one could fall in. Not to be outdone the people of
London had taken to the Thames in boats and barges and sailed
up and down trying to catch a glimpse of the proceedings. It was
estimated that as many as 6000 people had turned out to see the
new queen.

As Henry rode out his trumpeters announced his coming.
They were followed by members of the king's council and
the privy chamber, nobles of the realm, bishops and foreign
dignitaries and finally the king.

His persone was apparelled in a coate of purple velvet, somewhat
made lyke a frocke, all over embroidered with flatte golde of Damaske
wih small lace mixed between of the same gold and other laces of the
same so goyng traverse wyse, that the ground little appered: about
whiche garment was a ryche garde very curiously embroidered,
the sleves and brest were cut, lined with cloth of golde, and tied
together with great buttons of Diamondes, Rubyes and Orient

Perle, his sworde and swordgyrdle adorned with stones and especial
Emerodes, his night cappe garnished with stone, but his bonnet was
so ryche of Juels that fewe men coulde value them. Beside all this he
ware in baudrike wyse a coller of such Balistes and Perle that few
men ever sawe the lyke.[16]

Anne too had dressed in a fine gown of cloth of gold in the
German fashion with a cap of pearls and her hair covered in
black velvet. Jewels adorned her neck and she looked every inch
a queen albeit a foreign one. Marillac, the French ambassador,
thought she looked older than her twenty-four years nor was she
'so beautiful as everyone affirmed. She is tall and very assured in
carriage and countenance, showing that in her turn and vivacity
of wit supplies the place of beauty. She brings from her brother's
country 12 or 15 damsels inferior in beauty even to their mistress
and dressed so heavily and unbecomingly that they would be
thought ugly even if they were beautiful'.[17]

Anne rode out to meet the king. It's hard to guess which one
of them was dreading this meeting more. Anne was anxious but
may not have any idea of how much Henry disliked her at this
point. He acted with honour, saluted and embraced her and Anne
made a short speech in English that she had well-rehearsed.
They rode on to Greenwich Palace. The chronicler Hall was so
spellbound he wrote 'Oh! what a sight was this, to see so goodly
a prince and so noble a king to ride with so fair a lady, of so
goodly a stature, and so womanly a countenance, and in especial
of so good qualities; I think no creature could see them but his
heart rejoiced'. Once there Henry embraced Anne again and led
her to the queen's apartments. Then he went to find Cromwell.

Their wedding was supposed to take place the next day but
Henry now frantically sought a way out. He admitted Anne was
'well and seemly'[18] but he had no wish to marry her. Calling
his council, he ordered them to find a way to put a stop to it.
Perhaps Anne's pre-contract with the Duke of Lorraine could

be used as a way out. The Cleves ambassadors headed by Olisleger were called to clarify the matter but asked to speak to the Council the next morning so they could prepare their response. More than anything they were shocked to have been asked for documentation of a pre-contact that had already been discussed and found invalid. Did Anne have any idea as she sat at the evening banquet dressed in a gown trimmed with sable, her expensive cap covered in jewels and pearls, that Henry was trying his hardest to wrangle out of making her his bride?

Her ambassadors met with the council the next day and declared that the pre-contact between Anne and the Duke of Lorraine had been revoked but they had no proof. They had brought no documentation with them and it could be up to three months before it arrived. Olisleger said they would stay as hostages until that time.

Cromwell hurried to tell Henry who felt it was not 'well handled' and said:

> *If it were not that she is come so far into my realm and the great preparations that my states and my people have made for her and for fear of making a ruffle in the world – that is to mean to drive her brother into the hands of the Emperor and the French king's hands, being now together, I would never have her, but now it is so far gone.*[19]

The situation was too far gone and this wasn't just about Henry and whether he thought Anne was attractive or not. He could not afford to upset the German alliance. But perhaps the lady would admit herself that she was betrothed to Lorraine? Henry's final hope for getting out of the wedding. Dashed when Anne declared 'that she was free from all contracts'[20] and her ambassadors too signed to swear that the pre-contract was null and void.

Henry is said to have cried when he heard the news 'Is there none other Remedy, but that I must needs, against my will, put my neck in the yoke?' There wasn't and Henry found himself signing Anne's jointures detailing the properties she would receive as queen and sulkily preparing for his wedding the next day.

Henry was up and ready early, dressed in a gown of cloth of gold and rich black fur with a coat of crimson satin fastened with large diamonds, but swearing to Cromwell like a petulant child that 'if it were not to satisfy the world and my realm, I would not do that I must do this day for none earthly thing'.[21] Anne took longer to prepare for the ceremony that would change her life. There was a delay whilst they waited for the Earl of Essex who was to lead her up the aisle with Ambassador Overstein. Cromwell was about to take his place when he arrived and escorted Anne dressed in cloth of gold, embroidered with flowers of pearls, to her wedding. She kept her hair loose and flowing as was custom crowned with a gold coronet fashioned to look like sprigs of rosemary. On seeing Henry she curtseyed to him three times and they proceeded to the Queen's Closet where Archbishop Cranmer was waiting to perform the ceremony. Henry placed her wedding ring on her finger. It had the inscription 'God send me well to keep'.

After they heard mass, light refreshment of hypocras was served and Henry left to change into a gown of tissue lined with embroidered crimson velvet before rejoining Anne for their wedding banquet. Later Anne and her ladies also changed their clothes for gowns only fashionable in Germany. It was said Anne had 'a gown like a man's, furred with rich sables'.[22] After evensong, there was entertainment and feasting and then it was time for bed.

We can only feel for Anne. This was her wedding night, an experience perhaps to dread, but her duty to her new husband. Her mother must have told her something about what to expect and she must have been scared and apprehensive. Henry of course had no wish to go through with such a chore and there was a distinct lack of bedding ceremony revels. The marriage remained unconsummated. Raging at Cromwell the next morning when asked if he liked the queen:

Surely, my lord, I liked her before not well, but now I like her much worse! She is nothing fair, and have very evil smells about her. I took her to be no maid by reason of the looseness of her breasts and other tokens, which, when I felt them, strake me so to the heart, that I had neither will nor courage to prove the rest. I can have none appetite for displeasant airs. I have left her as good a maid as I found her.[23]

Henry may have purposely restrained from consummation on the first night while he still considered ways to get out of his marriage. It was also the Feast of the Epiphany and it was believed that children conceived on that day could be 'lepers, epileptics or possessed by the devil'.[24] We don't know if Anne was completely bewildered by her wedding night or relieved. Henry was by now obese and ungainly and his attempts at fumbling her body must have been borne through gritted teeth. Though to anyone who saw the comings and goings of the court all was going well. Henry presented her with *morgengabe* gifts, a German custom, of lavish dresses, pearl rings and jewel studded belts and plans were under way for jousts and entertainment in Anne's honour.

But Henry was on his way to consult with his doctors. Dr John Chamber advised him 'not to enforce himself, for eschewing such inconveniences as by debility ensuing in that case were to be feared'[25] so he refrained from any attempt at sexual relations on the second night. He tried on the third and fourth night but could not go through with it. There had been rumours about the king's impotency when he was married to Anne Boleyn and he was eager to make the doctors understand that the problem was not with him. It was all Anne's fault 'her body in such sort disordered and indisposed to excite and provoke any lust'.[26] He had had two wet dreams so he knew he was functioning normally. He would continue to sleep with Anne without any sexual contact for months.

Her ladies would later testify that they asked Anne whether she was pregnant or not. When Anne insisted she wasn't, they teased her for being a maid. To which she is supposed to have replied 'How can I be a maid, and sleep every night with the king? When he comes to bed he kisses me and taketh me by the hand and biddeth me "Goodnight sweetheart" and in the morning kisses me and biddeth me "Farewell darling". Is this not enough?' to which Lady Rutland responded 'Madam, there must be more, or it will be long ere we have a Duke of York, which all this realm most desireth'. Anne was 'contented' she knew 'no more'.[27] Given this testimony was given during later proceedings, it is hard to believe that Anne was so naïve. She also spoke very little English at the time so it would be hard for her to have had such a conversation.

Regardless of whether this conversation truly occurred, Anne by now couldn't fail to notice something was amiss and she frequently tried to speak with Cromwell. When the minister told the king, Henry thought it a good idea that Cromwell should give her some advice but he baulked at so delicate a conversation. Instead he tried to pass it on to the Earl of Rutland, her lord chamberlain and the Queen's Council. He asked Rutland to 'find some means that the Queen might be induced to order (her) Grace pleasantly in her behaviour towards (the king), thinking thereby for to have had some faults amended' and the Council to 'counsel their mistress to use all pleasantness to (the king)'.[28] But whether any of these men broached the subject with the new queen is doubtful.

On 11 January a joust was held in Anne's honour. Henry no longer competed after his accident in 1536 but he still enjoyed the spectacle. This time Anne dressed in an English gown with a French hood that had people commenting how much better it suited her than her heavy German gowns. Henry might not even have noticed. Anne was making an effort to fit in but the king was past caring whether she did or not.

According to Leti, an Italian historian, the Princess Elizabeth wrote to Anne, her new step-mother at this time:

Madame,—I am struggling between two contending wishes—one is my impatient desire to see your Majesty, the other that of rendering the obedience, I owe to the commands of the King my father, which prevent me from leaving my house till he has given me full permission to do so. But I hope that I shall be able shortly to gratify both these desires. In the meantime, I entreat your Majesty to permit me to show, by this billet, the zeal with which I devote my respect to you as my queen, and my entire obedience to you as to my mother. I am too young and feeble to have power to do more than to felicitate you with all my heart in this commencement of your marriage. I hope that your Majesty will have as much good will for me as I have zeal for your service.[29]

Anne showed the letter to the king and asked that Elizabeth be allowed to come to court but Henry would have none of it. He told Cromwell to write back to her 'that she had a mother so different from this woman that she ought not to wish to see her'.[30] Unfortunately this letter no longer exists so cannot be corroborated but there does seem to have been some altercation between Anne and the king over the Princess Mary. Both of the king's daughters had not been invited to the wedding or following celebrations and it is safe to say they wished to meet their new stepmother. Henry complained to Cromwell that he 'hadde sume communicacyon with her of my ladye Marye how that she began to wax stoborne and wylfull'.[31] Not only did he find Anne unattractive but she had had the temerity to argue with him.

But Henry kept up the pretence that all was well writing to Anne's brother William promising that he would 'act sincerely in matters concerning their friendship and the marriage'.[32] Wotton was sent to Cleves with the king's dispatches and to assure the duke and his mother that everything was just fine. He arrived before the Cleves ambassadors returned home and with them news of Henry's wish to see Anne's pre-contact documentation. Henry had richly rewarded them with gifts of money and plate and Anne had said her goodbyes. Some of her ladies were also due to return. Lady Keteler was sent back with a message from Anne to her mother and brother to thank them 'most heartily for having preferred her to such a marriage that she could wish no better'.[33] Mother Lowe stayed with her to supervise her remaining German maids and her new English ones with Count von Waldeck also staying to help her acclimatise to her new country.

Although her relationship with the king left much to be desired, Anne was embracing her role as queen and adapting to living in England. She was learning the language, listening to music, especially that played by the Bassano family, walking in the gardens, practising her cross-stitch or cushion stitch 'opus pulvinarium' (introducing German designs into England) and enjoying the company of her ladies with whom she played cards or dice.

No date had been set for her coronation although Marillac, the French ambassador, had heard it would be in May. Henry was stalling but he did arrange for Anne's state entry into Westminster on 4 February. Taking separate barges and accompanied by their households, guards and the Mayor and Aldermen of London in other vessels they left Greenwich for Westminster along the Thames.

First, his Graces (household) going in barges afore his Majesty, then his Grace going in his barge and his gard following in another barge; then the Quene in her barg and her ladies following in another barge, and then her household servants, then the Mayor and the Aldermen of London in a barge and tenne of the cheiffe craftes of the cities following the mayor in their barges, which were all rychlie hanged with schuchions and targattes and banners of the cognisans of everie occupation, the Mercers barge hanged rychlie with cloath of gold' and from Greenwych to the Towre all the shipps which laie in the Thames shott gonnes as the kinge and queene passed by them. And when they came against the Tower their was shott within the Tower above a thousand chambers of ordinance which made a noyse like thunder; and that donne they passed through London Bridge to Westminster, the mayor and all the craftes following till they see their Grace on land, which was first coming of the Queenes Grace to Westminster synce her Graces coming into Englande.[34]

Henry helped Anne disembark and led her to Whitehall Palace. In his heart he knew that Anne would never be crowned queen.

SIR THOMAS CROMWELL KNIGHT etc.

SIR THOMAS CROMWELL KNIGHT &c.   HEE LIVED IN K. HENRY THE 8
time. beeing a Blackſmiths ſonne borne at Putney;   But by the Vertue of his ſingu
lar excellencie of wilt, beeing fit & able to order any weighty affairs, hee attained by de
grees to the dignity of Lord Keeper of y privy Seale; E of the Garter; then created Earle of Eſſex,
& high Chamberlaine of Englad,   at laſt the king Vicegerent in all matters Eccleſiaſticall;
Wherfore in Parliament hee hadt the precedence of Biſh of Canter; by means whereof hee
ſupprest all Monaſteries & Friars, & defaced all ſhrines and Images & ſuchlike;   Laſtly
hee was attaint by the Parliament & accuſed of treaſon & Hereſie, as ſupporter of the Lutherians;
then was beheaded on the Towerhill, the 28 of July 1540.

Thomas Cromwell

60

Chapter Five

Cromwell's Defeat
1540

In March Anne received a visit from Karl Harst, the new ambassador from Cleves. He arrived without any of the pre-contract documentation as requested by the king, spoke only Latin and not English, only had one servant and was poorly dressed. Her brother William had seemingly not well provisioned the envoy perhaps feeling that now Anne was married, the situation was unimportant. He had much more to worry about with Charles V pressing his right to Guelders. Now Henry had married into Cleves he would be expected to aid Anne's brother if hostilities broke out and that was something the king had no intention of doing. Wotton was instructed to keep the king informed of a changing situation and advise William to avert war.

Anne had accompanied Henry to Hampton Court for Easter and returned to Westminster for the opening of the third session of the seventh parliament on 12 April which included amongst items to by discussed – the dissolution of their marriage. Cromwell, who was charged with finding a way out of the nuptials that he had brokered, was made Earl of Essex and Lord Great Chamberlain on 18 April. Henry might have thought that raising him higher would give him incentive to sort out his 'secret matter' or perhaps he relished the greater fall Cromwell would make if he disappointed him. Certainly others were aware of Cromwell's precarious position. Marillac reported he was 'tottering' and that if he remained 'in his former credit and authority it will only be because he is very assiduous in affairs, although rough in his management of them, and that he does nothing without first consulting the king'.[1]

After Cromwell's elevation the king joined Anne in the Queen's apartments for dinner. Anne might not have known that things had progressed so far but she knew something was afoot. Lady Lisle was stilling trying to gain a place for her daughter Katherine in Anne's household. Her daughter Anne Basset told her that the king wanted only those 'that should be fair'.[3] Katherine was obviously not pretty enough to catch the king's eye as her sister had once done. Her husband had approached Olisleger who had informed him 'I am sorry to tell you that, having spoken, with the Queen's good will, to the King and my lord Privy Seal to have your wife's daughter Katherine in the Queen's privy chamber, I have been answered that the ladies of the privy chamber were appointed before the coming of Madame; and though I have begged that an exception might be made in her favor, it has been of no avail'.[2] When she tried again she was told that no more maids would be employed. Henry had no reason to expand the queen's household and was instead hoping to disband it as soon as possible. One of the queen's maids had already caught his eye and Anne had noticed. The teenage Katherine Howard, the Duke of Norfolk's niece and Anne Boleyn's cousin, had joined Anne's household in January and by April the king was granting her land and arranging for her to receive a gift of quilted sarcanet. Henry was nothing if not generous to his mistress and rumours soon abounded about the king's affection for this slight, immature young girl.

On 1 May five days of jousting at Westminster, the last of Henry's reign, were accompanied by nightly banquets at Durham house. It was a fantastic spectacle – the knights 'rytchlie apparayled and their horses trapped, all in white velvett, with certaine knightes and gentlemen riding afore them apparayled all in white velvett and white sarcenett, and all their servantes in white sarcenet dobletts and hosin, after the Burgonion fashion'[4] but it would also be the last time that Henry and Anne appeared together as king and queen. Anne however was oblivious to

Henry's machinations to end their marriage and sent Karl Harst to enquire when her coronation would be.

Cromwell knew Henry would never be happy until Anne was gone. Talking to Wriothesley he complained 'The King liketh not the Queen, nor ever has from the beginning; I think assuredly she is as good a maid for him as she was when she came to England'.[5] Wriothesely urged him to 'devise relief for the king'.[6] He knew that if the king was not appeased soon, Cromwell would be in trouble.

As the king's minister left parliament on 10 June his hat blew off in the wind. It was usual for those present to doff their caps in respect but no one moved to remove their hats. At the dinner that followed no one spoke to Cromwell and when he joined Henry's counsellors for a meeting he found them all seated. Going to take his place Norfolk broke the silence 'Cromwell, do not sit there; that is no place for thee. Traitors do not sit amongst gentlemen'.[7] He was arrested by the captain of the guard and stripped of his garter seal and insignia before being taken to the Tower of London.

On 12 June Cromwell wrote a long letter to Henry from the tower. It covered all he had been accused of including revealing the king's matter with the queen:

Most gracious King and most merciful sovereign, your most humble, most obedient and most bounden subject and most lamentable servant and prisoner. Prostrate at the feet of your most excellent Majesty, I have heard your pleasure by the mouth of your Controller, which was that I should write to your most excellent Highness such things as I thought meet to be written concerning my most miserable state and condition...

Amongst other things, most gracious sovereign, Master Controller showed me that you complained that within these 14 days I revealed a matter of great secrecy contrary to your expectation. Sire, I do well remember the matter, but I never revealed it to any creature except after your Grace had opened the matter first to me in your chamber decrying your lamentable fate. You declared the thing which your Highness misliked in the Queen, at which time I told your Grace that she often desired to speak with me but I durst not. You said why should I not, alleging that I might do much good in going to her and to be plain with her in declaring my mind. Lacking opportunity, I spoke with her lord Chamberlain, for which I ask your Grace's mercy, desiring him – not naming your Grace to him – to find some means that the Queen might be induced to behave pleasantly towards you. I thought thereby to have some faults amended to your Majesty's comfort. I repeated the suggestion, when the said lord Chamberlain and others of the Queen's council came to me in my chamber at Westminster for licence for the departure of the strange maidens. I then required them to counsel their mistress to use all pleasantness to your Highness. This was before your Grace committed the secret matter to me, and only so that she might have been induced to such pleasant and honorable fashions as might have been to your Grace's comfort which above all things, as God knoweth, I did most court and desire. After that time, I never disclosed to any but my lord Admiral, which I did by your Grace's commandment on Sunday last; whom I found equally willing to seek a remedy for your comfort and consolation. I saw by him that he did as much lament your Highness' fate as ever did man, and was wonderfully grieved to see your Highness so troubled, wishing greatly your comfort and saying he would spend the best blood in his belly for that object. And if I would not do the same and willingly die for your comfort, I would I were in Hell and I receive a thousand deaths. Sire, this is all that I have done in this matter and if I have offended your Majesty therein, prostrate at your feet I most lowly ask mercy and pardon of your Highness.[8]

Only Cranmer stood up for him writing to the king:

I heard yesterday in your Grace's Council, that he [Crumwell] is a traitor, yet who cannot be sorrowful and amazed that he should be a traitor against your Majesty, he that was so advanced by your Majesty … I loved him as my friend, for so I took him to be; but I chiefly loved him for the love which I thought I saw him bear ever towards your Grace, singularly above all other. But now, if he be a traitor, I am sorry that ever I loved him or trusted him, and I am very glad that his treason is discovered in time; but yet again I am very sorrowful; for who shall your Grace trust hereafter, if you might not trust him?[9]

Neither the letters Cromwell wrote or Cranmer's words would dissuade Henry from seeing the man condemned. The king had grown weary of waiting for Cromwell to find a way out of his Cleves marriage and the minister's enemies had convinced the king that he never would. On 19 June an act of attainder was passed declaring Cromwell guilty with no recourse to a trial. All Henry wanted now was Cromwell's account of his involvement in his marriage to Anne. In that he hoped to find evidence for annulment. Cromwell duly wrote down all his thoughts and feelings but nothing he did would save him from the executioner's block.

Anne must have been shocked and dismayed to hear of Cromwell's downfall and if nothing had alerted her to her precarious position before now she had every reason to become anxious. More of Anne's ladies returned to Germany in June. William Paget accompanied them with a letter from Henry to Anne's mother detailing how well they had served the queen but Anne's circle was getting smaller and she had no support from any of the nobles at court. She complained to Harst, her brother's ambassador, about Katherine Howard and knew that as Katherine of Aragon and Anne Boleyn had been put aside for a lady-in-waiting so might she.

Others had also noticed Henry's new infatuation and pondered what it meant for the queen. Richard Hilles wrote to a contemporary:

> *Before St. John Baptist's day [24th June] it was whispered the King intended to divorce his queen Anne, sister of the duke of Gelderland, whom he had married publicly at Epiphany after last Christmas. Courtiers first observed that he was much taken with another young lady, very small of stature, whom he now has, and whom he was seen crossing the Thames to visit, often in the day time and sometimes at night. The bp. of Winchester provided feastings for them in his palace, but it was looked upon as a sign of adultery, not of divorce.*[10]

When Anne received a message from the council that she was to retire to Richmond Palace she became frightened. Harst tried to comfort her and convince her it was for the best but was worried for her state of mind and sent to Cleves to inform them and ask that they wrote to her for support. This removal from court was seemingly 'for her health, open air and pleasure'[11] because there was plague in London. Henry promised to join her in a few days but of course he didn't. He would have soon moved if the plague was really a problem 'for he is the most timid person in the world in such cases'.[12] Instead he stayed in the city where it was easier for him to visit the lovely Katherine most evenings. Anne waited anxiously at the beautiful red bricked palace of Richmond rebuilt after the fire of 1497, with its stunning gardens on the edge of the River Thames, close to a deer park and hunting grounds. Her surroundings may have been beautiful but she spent her first days here afraid for her life, anxiously awaiting news from the king.

Henry now tasked Stephen Gardiner, Bishop of Winchester, with furthering the inquiry into the legality of his marriage. On 29 June he set out a memorandum for the council detailing the process and the points that needed to be examined. It mostly focused on Anne's pre-contract to the Duke of Lorraine and the nonconsummation of the king and queen's nuptials. Cromwell needed to be interrogated, documents assembled, the queen told and her permission gained for further inquiry by the church. The details that Henry had required from Cleves of the repudiation of Anne's pre-contract, the 'beer pot' document, is noted in Letters and Papers in February but it seems this may be misleading as no attention was paid to it until now. It was signed in Cleves on 26 February 1540 with a beer pot seal so it must have arrived in the intervening months. Gardiner felt it 'containeth no m(anner) of discharge at all, but rather ministerth matter of m(uch doubt.'[13]

On 6 July, Anne was rudely awoken in the early hours of the morning with a message from the king carried by Beard. She immediately sent for Harst to explain it to her. She was informed that her consent was needed for an inquiry into the validity of her marriage to be conducted by clergymen (thus taking the blame from Henry). The Earl of Rutland, Anne's lord chamberlain, joined them and 'did see her take the matter heavily' so he 'desired her to be of good comfort'[14] and assured her that the king had her best interests at heart so she had 'cause to rejoice and not be sorry'.[15] Anne took the news stoically and made no reply to Rutland but knowing the fate of her predecessors felt terrible fear for her future. The king needed a reply however and she gave Beard her consent but would not write anything down. Harst was beside himself with anger and refused to take any written acceptance to the king but as soon as it was light he rushed to court to find out what was going on. In an audience with Henry's councillors he was assured that the inquiry was merely to quash rumours and Anne would be treated according to her position. He asked that proceedings be delayed until more ambassadors arrived from Cleves but of course Henry had no time for that.

The same day the Lord Chancellor, the Archbishop of Canterbury, the Bishop of Durham, the Dukes of Norfolk and Suffolk and the Earl of Southampton informed the House of

Lords that there was reason to question the validity of the king's marriage and to ask for an ecclesiastical inquiry. Receiving a positive reply, the convocation would begin the next day. A delegation of the Privy Council was sent to Anne to explain more fully the situation to her and they reported to the king that she was 'content always with your majesty'.[16] They were good to go ahead.

There was never really going to be any other result rather than what the king wanted and despite Harst's protests about Anne's mistreatment and the fact she was not called to give evidence nor shown any of the documentation and statements, the convocation of clergy took three days to find their marriage invalid on the grounds of Anne's pre-contract to the Duke of Lorraine, on Henry's lack of consent and lack of consummation in what Burnet described as 'the greatest piece of compliance that ever the King had from the clergy'.[17] Henry had had his back-up plan of 'secret causes' at the ready if they needed any more convincing but in the end he did not have to disclose what would touch 'the honour of the lady'[18] probably alluding to the fact that after Henry had run his hands over her body he perceived her not to be a maiden.

Anne may have been happy not to have had to attend and hear her private life exposed by witnesses including her own ladies and Henry's doctors but Harst, in his correspondence back to Cleves, gave a picture of a lady not quite as acquiescing to the whole affair as Henry would have liked. Anne was no fool and knew the trip from the palace at Richmond to the Tower of London was not far. Henry may have executed Anne Boleyn but she was English and without support by the time of her fall, Anne was German and to upset Cleves and its supporters was another matter altogether. Still Anne could not risk making a fuss even though her life was in turmoil.

A parliamentary statement was made:

We consider your majesty not bound by the pretensed marriage, which is of itself nought and of no force, so your majesty, without tarrying for any judgement may contract and consummate matrimony with any other woman. The Lady Anne did of her own free will assent and has openly confessed that she remains not carnally known of the King's body. She has also signified her confession by a letter subscribed in her own hand. And the Lady Anne shall not be named or called the King's wife.[19]

It sounded so simple but Anne had in fact been distraught by the findings she was no longer queen of England. Some reports said she fainted on hearing the news that her marriage was over and Harst reported during the deliberations and days of waiting she had cried and wept so violently it near broke his heart. As far as Henry was concerned 'she was troubled and perplexed, in consequence of the great love and affection which she seemed to have only to our person'.[20]

On July 11 Anne wrote to the king:

Pleaseth your most excellent majesty to understand that, whereas, at sundry times heretofore, I have been informed and perceived by certain lords and others your grace's council, of the doubts and questions which have been moved and found in our marriage; and how hath petition thereupon been made to your highness by your nobles and commons, that the same might be examined and determined by the holy clergy of this realm; to testify to your highness by my writing, that which I have before promised by my word and will, that is to say, that the matter should be examined and determined by the said clergy; it may please your majesty to know that, though this case must needs be most hard and sorrowful unto me, for the great love which I bear to your most noble person, yet, having more regard to God and his truth than to any worldly affection, as it beseemed me, at the beginning, to submit me to such examination and determination of the said clergy, whom I have and do accept for judges competent in that behalf. So now being ascertained how the same clergy hath therein given their judgment and sentence, I acknowledge myself hereby to accept and approve the same, wholly and entirely putting myself, for my state and condition, to your highness' goodness and pleasure; most humbly beseeching your majesty that, though it be determined that the pretended matrimony between us is void and of none effect, whereby I neither can nor will repute myself for your grace's wife, considering this sentence (whereunto I stand) and your majesty's clean and pure living with me, yet it will please you to take me for one of your humble servants, and so determine of me, as I may sometimes have the fruition of your most noble presence; which as I shall esteem for a great benefit, so, my lords and others of your majesty's council, now being with me, have put me in comfort thereof; and that your highness will take me for your sister; for the which I most humbly thank you accordingly.[21]

And she signed it 'Your majesty's most humble sister and servant, Anne the daughter of Cleves'.

Anne's agreement to the annulment was announced in parliament and the same day the Duke of Suffolk, Earl of Southampton, and Wriothesley met with Anne and delivered the terms of her settlement. Henry would be 'a perfect friend, content to repute you as our dearest sister'[22] as long as she agreed to the terms. Her allowance would be £4000 a year in revenues from estates and lands across the country including Hever Castle, Anne Boleyn's childhood home, with £500 income plus she could keep Richmond Palace and Bletchingley Manor in Surrey as her homes. She was allowed her jewels and dresses, hangings, furniture and plate and there would be money for keeping her household. Her role as 'sister' would give her precedence over all the ladies at court except the queen and the king's daughters. It was a generous settlement and more than Anne had hoped for. 'But where was Bletchingley?' she enquired of the councillors fearful of being shunted off to a dank, dark dwelling as Katherine of Aragon had been. Bletchingley was about eighteen miles outside of London and had been forfeited to the crown on the execution of Sir Nicholas Carew. It was surrounded by parkland and so would be a suitable accommodation for the sister of the king, Anne was assured. There was a gift too of 500 marks for her compliance.

After receiving Anne's letter Henry wrote back to her:

Right dear and right entirely beloved sister,

By the relation of the lord Master, lord Privy Seal and others of our Council lately addressed unto you we perceive the continuance of your conformity, which before was reported, and by your letters is eftsoons testified. We take your wise and honourable proceedings therein in most thankful part, as it is done in respect of God and his trust, and, continuing your conformity, you shall find us a perfect friend, content to repute you as our dearest sister. We shall, within five or six days, when our Parliament ends, determine your state after such honourable sort as you shall have good cause to be content, we minding to endow you with £4000 of yearly revenue. We have appointed you two houses, that at Richmond where you now lie, and the other at Bletchingley, not far from London that you may be near us and, as you desire, able to repair to Court to see us, as we shall repair to you. When Parliament ends, we shall, in passing, see and speak with you, and you shall more largely see what a friend you and your friends have of us. Be quiet and merry.[23]

Be quiet and merry indeed. Anne had agreed to everything and Henry could sigh with relief and now make plans to marry his next queen. But Anne wasn't so complaint about everything. Henry asked that she contact her brother William, Duke of Cleves, to explain the situation but Anne did not think it appropriate that she wrote to him first nor did she really want to let her family know of the failure of her marriage for the shame and embarrassment it would cause her. But it had to be done and after a few days Anne finally penned her heartfelt letter.

My dear and well-beloved brother, — After my most hearty commendation. Whereas, by your letters of the 13th of this month, which I have seen, written to the king's majesty of England, my most dear and most kind brother, I do perceive you take the matter, lately moved and determined between him and me, somewhat to heart. Forasmuch as I had rather ye knew the truth by mine advertisement, than for want thereof ye should be deceived by vain reports. I thought mete to write these present letters to you, by the which it shall please you to understand, how the nobles and commons of this realm desired the king's highness to commit the examination of the matter of marriage between his majesty and me to the determination of the holy clergy of this realm. I did then willingly consent thereto; and since their determination made, have also, upon intimation of their proceedings, allowed, approved, and agreed to the same.[25]

She went on to tell William that Henry had adopted her as his sister and that he 'as a most kind, loving and friendly brother useth me, was as much or more humanity and liberality, as you, I myself, or any of our kin or allies, could well wish or desire'.[26] The Duke of Cleves was of course unhappy with the situation. He had been informed of the inquiry into the legality of the marriage but refused to accept the divorce. Anne had taken pains to also send a verbal message with her official letter via Olisleger's nephew who was tasked to take the missive to Cleves. She was extremely anxious that her family would bear her no ill will. William for his part did not blame her and even suggested she could return to Cleves but Anne's settlement depended on her staying in England and Anne also knew that by staying in England she had status, property and money while returning to Cleves would leave her with nothing.

On 17 July Anne's household was changed. The servants who attended her were reduced from over 100 to 30. Many of her ladies were discharged and would ultimately go on to serve the next queen. Lady Lisle finally got her wish and her daughter Katherine Basset gained a place in Anne's new household and would be joined by Dorothy Wingfield, Frances Lilgrave, Jane Ratsey and a Mrs. Sympson whilst Anne still kept two of the original ladies, Katherine and Gertrude, that had come to England with her. Sir William Goring was now her chamberlain, Wymond Carew her receiver and Jasper Horsey her steward at Richmond. Thomas Cawarden was made keeper and steward of Anne's new residence at Bletchingley. Their fractious relationship would last for many years.

A warrant for payment of their wages included several 'strangers' who were men of Cleves still in Anne's service including Gymmech Shenck, Groisbeck Vresvydour, Dr. Cornelis (Cepher), physician, Mathyew, secretary, Schoulenburg, the cook, Henry the butler and her footmen. Warner van Gymnych, her cup-bearer was earning extra by exporting 800 tuns of beer but others were not so happy with their wages.

Wymond Carew was earning £20 a year, £6 less than Jasper Horsey and he wrote to John Gate of the King's Privy Chamber to complain and seek an increase.

I pray you learn of my lord Privy Seal whether I and my wife shall have the same allowance as Mr. Horssey and his wife have, for I think myself no meaner than he. If his lordship seem not so to esteem me, get my brother Deny to despatch me hence, for the lady Anne of Clevelond is bent to do me displeasure. I think she has heard how I procured the knowledge of such letters as were sent to her, which of truth at the beginning she denied. She esteems my wife two degrees under Mrs. Horssey.

P.S. — She had a letter three days past from her Grace's brother, and because she did not seem minded to send it to the King I asked her brother's ambassador whether she had had any, and he said they were letters of congratulation from her brother. I further told him he should advise her to send them to the King. I was commanded by my lord of Suffolk to show the King's Council what letters were sent to her, and I have moved her chamberlain so to do, who has so moved her.[26]

It is obvious that he felt Anne was doing him and his family a disservice and not listening to his complaint about wages but as we can see from the rest of this note he was actually spying on Anne and informing the king of any letters she received. It did not endear him to her and when she received correspondence from her brother she sent it directly to the king rather than have Carew inform on her.

The councillors returned to Richmond on the 21st to bring Anne gifts from the king and show her letters 'as, by the Bishop's letter, it seemed that Olisleger feared she was not well treated'.[27] She wrote in her own language to her brother:

Brother, Because I had rather ye know the truth by mine advertisement, than for want thereof be deceived by false reports, I write these present letters to you, by which ye shall understand that being advertised how the nobles and commons of this realm, desired the king's highness here, to commit the examination of the matter of marriage between me and his majesty to the determination of the clergy, I did the more willingly consent thereto; and since the determination made, have also allowed, approved, and agreed unto the same, wherein I have more respect (as becometh me) to truth and good pleasure than any worldly affection that might move me to the contrary. I account God pleased with what is done, and know myself to have suffered no wrong or injury, my person being preserved in the integrity which I brought into this realm, and I truly discharged from all bond of consent. I find the king's highness, whom I cannot justly have as my husband, to be, nevertheless, a most kind, loving and friendly father and brother, and to use me as honourably, and with as much liberality, as you, I myself, or any of our kin or allies, could wish; wherein l am, for mine own part, so well content and satisfied, that I much desire my mother, you, and other, mine allies, so to understand, accept, and take it, and so to use yourself towards this noble and virtuous prince, as he may have cause to continue his friendship towards you, which on his behalf shall nothing be impaired or altered in this matter—for so it hath pleased his highness to signify to me, that like as he will show to me always a most fatherly and brotherly kindness, and has so provided for me, so will he remain with you and other, according to the knot of amity which between you hath been concluded (this matter notwithstanding), in such wise as neither I, ne you, nor any of our friends, shall have just cause of miscontentment. Thus much I have thought necessary to write to you, lest, for want of true knowledge, ye might take this matter otherwise than ye ought, and in other sort care for me than ye have cause. Only I require this of you, that ye so conduct yourself as for your untowardness in this matter, I fare not the worse, whereunto I trust you will have regard.[28]

This message was not just for William but for her sister Sybilla and her husband John Frederick who after years of stalled negotiations with Henry over his admission to the Schmalkaldic League, was furious and wanted no more to do with the king. Anne feared their retaliation and urged them to caution. She was happy with her settlement and wanted nothing more than to be left in peace. Across Europe the news of Henry and Anne's annulment sent shockwaves through courts and commoners alike. Anne had the sympathy of the people but also a lucky escape. As a final gesture she sent her wedding ring back to Henry 'desiring that it might be broken in pieces as a thing which she knew of no force or value'.[29]

On July 28 Cromwell was executed. It was a stark warning to Anne that those who displeased the king suffered with their own lives. Henry, forever the master of inappropriate timing, married Katherine Howard secretly at Oatlands Palace the same day. Katherine was the daughter of Lord Edmund Howard and Joyce Culpeper but after her mother's death had been raised in the Dowager Duchess of Norfolk's undisciplined and some would say scandalous household. Henry was utterly besotted with her. She was everything Anne was not. Young, beautiful and lively but with only one portrait of her historians have differed in their description of her. Starkey describes her as having 'auburn hair, pale skin, dark eyes and brows, the rather fetching beginnings of a double chin and an expression that was at once quizzical and come-hither'[30] whilst Denny describes her as 'demure and dainty, with peaches-and-cream complexion and blonde hair'.[31] Marillac writing at the time said she 'had everything necessary not only to content the king her lord, but also to win the hearts of his subjects; for, apart from her excellent beauty in which she surpassed all the ladies in England... she has a very gentle face, gracious of speech, her bearing moderate, restrained and her conversation humane'.[32] But she would drive the king to distraction.

However in the early days of their marriage all was well. The king had not forgotten his fourth wife and visited Anne on 6 August to tell her of his marriage. As Marillac reported:

This King being lately with a small company at Hampton Court, ten miles hence, supped at Richmond with the Queen that was, so merrily that some thought he meant to reinstate her, but others think it was done to get her consent to the dissolution of the marriage and make her subscribe what she had said thereupon, which is not only what they wanted but also what she thinks they expected. The latter opinion is the more likely, as the King drew her apart in company with the three first councillors he had, who are not commonly called in to such confidences. Thinks it would show great inconstancy to take her back now, and moreover she did not sup with him as she did when she was Queen, but at another table adjoining his, as other ladies who are not of the blood do when he eats in company.[33]

The French ambassador also reported how joyous Anne had become and that she wore different dresses every day. Anne was happy at Richmond and was now one of the richest ladies in the kingdom.

Richmond Palace

Chapter Six

A New Queen Katherine
1541

Anne had been living the quiet life during the first few months of Henry's marriage to the young Katherine Howard but on 3 January she travelled to Hampton Court for the New Year celebrations. Her gift to the newlyweds were two horses with 'violet velvet trappings'.[1] She was welcomed at court by 'the duchess of Suffolk, the countess of Hertford, and certain other ladies, who, after conducting her to the rooms destined for her lodging, took her to the queen's apartments'.[2]

Both Anne and Katherine had been anxious about this meeting but Anne conducted herself 'with as much reverence and punctilious ceremony, as if she were herself the most insignificant damsel at court, all the time addressing the queen on her knees, notwithstanding the prayers and entreaties of the latter, who received her most kindly, showing her great favour and courtesy. At this time the king entered the room, and, after making a very low bow to Anne, embraced and kissed her'.[3]

Henry took his place next to Katherine at the top of the table. Anne sat at 'a seat near the bottom of the table, all the time keeping as good a mien and countenance, and looking as unconcerned as if there had been nothing between them'.[4] She spent the evening talking and dancing with the queen after Henry had retired. A year in England had passed and Anne had picked up more of the language and a lot of the customs, enough for the two women to spend a pleasant evening together. The next day the King sent Katherine a present of a ring and two small dogs, which she gave to Anne before she returned to Richmond. The two women were not recorded as ever seeing each other again.

All were delighted that the meeting of ex-queen and new

queen had gone so smoothly. Anne had accomplished the feat of truly acting like the king's sister. Not only was Henry pleased with her but he now gave her permission to see the Princess Elizabeth as she had previously requested with strict instructions that the princess must always refer to her as Lady Anne and never queen. Elizabeth was living a peripatetic life moving between Ashridge, Hatfield, Hunsdon, Enfield and Havering Bower so we are uncertain where they met. As later evidence shows she also nurtured a relationship with the Princess Mary, now welcome at court after a long estrangement with her father not helped by his marriage to a girl much younger than her and a relative of the hated Anne Boleyn no less.

Chapuys, the Spanish ambassador, who had staunchly supported Katherine of Aragon was back at court in July 1540 after several months' absence. Noted for his reports he was carefully watching how the new queen would fare. In May he wrote she was unhappy as she had heard rumours 'that he (the king) was about to take back Anne of Cleves as his wife. To which the king replied that she was wrong to believe such things (of him) or attach faith to reports of the kind; even if he had to marry again, he would never retake Mme. De Cleves'.[5] In fact rumours that the king might take Anne back started as early as October 1540 and would continue for quite some time. But the king was very much in love with Katherine and he wanted to show her to the nation. So at the end of June they set off on a royal progress into the North, culminating at York, taking the Princess Mary part of the way with them.

Hall recorded:

This Sommer the Kyng kepte his progresse to Yorke, and passed through Lyncolne Shire, where was made to hym an humble submission by the temporaltie, confessyng their offence, and thankyngthe kyng for his pardon: and the Toune of Staunforde gaue the Kyng twentie pounde, and Lyncolne presented fourtie pounde,

& Boston fiftie pound that parte whiche is called Lynsey gaue three
hundred pounde, and Kestren and the Churche of Lyncolne gaue
fiftie pounde. And when he entred into Yorke Shire, he was met
with two hundred gentlemen of the same Shire in coates of Veluet,
and foure thousande tall yornen, and seruyng men, well horsed:
whiche on their knees made a submission, by the mouthe of sir
Robert Bowes, and gaue to the Kyng nyne hundred pounde. And
on Barnesdale met the kyng, the Archebishoppe of Yorke, with three
hundred Priestes and more, and made a like submission, and gaue
the kyng sixe hundred pounde. Like submission was made by the
Maior of Yorke, Newe Castle and Hull, and eche of theim gaue to the
Kyng an hundred pounde. When the Kyng had been at Yorke twelue
daies, he came to Hull, and deuised there certain fortificacions, and
passed ouer the water of Homber, and so through Lyncolne Shire,
and at Halontidee came to Hampton Court.[6]

Anne of course was not invited. In the summer there were
two weddings that Anne could not attend but that nonetheless
interested her. The first was her brother William's marriage to
the twelve-year-old Jeanne of Navarre who although dressed in
a rich gold and silver skirt dotted with precious jewels and a
crimson cloak edged with ermine had to be carried to the altar
under protest. Francis I had arranged the marriage as part of a
peace treaty with the Duke of Cleves and as many women before
her Jeanne had to suffer a choice that was not hers. She wrote
down 'I, Jeanne de Navarre, persisting in the protestations I
have already made, do hereby again affirm and protest by these
present, that the marriage which it is desired to contract between
the Duke of Cleves and myself, is against my will; that I have
never consented to it, nor will consent...'[7] Not a happy start to
wedded bliss and like Anne's own marriage it would remain
unconsummated until its annulment.

The second was that of the Duke of Lorraine, her previously
betrothed, who now married Christina of Denmark in

Brussels. 'Great preparations had been made to do honour to the Emperor's niece, and the guests came from far and wide. Christina's trousseau was worthy of her exalted rank, and the Queen presented her with a wonderful carcanet of rubies, diamonds, and emeralds, with pendants of large pear-shaped pearls. The marriage was solemnized on Sunday, the 10th of July, in the great hall where, twenty-six years before, Isabella of Austria, had been married to the King of Denmark. Only two of the foreign Ambassadors were absent from the wedding banquet — the Englishmen Vaughan and Carne — a fact which naturally excited much comment. King Henry changed colour when Chapuys told him of Christina's marriage, and was at no pains to conceal his surprise and vexation'.[8]

Henry was not pleased. He had made much of wanting to marry Christina himself and spat 'I hold that Anne de Cleves is the real and legitimate wife of the said marquis, for I myself have never seen or heard of any deed or authentic documents breaking through their mutual marriage engagement that being the chief reason and cause of my separation from her'.[9] Of course it was one of the reasons for his divorce but as Henry was allowed to remarry so was Anne and the duke. The marriage of Francis and Christina was perfectly legal but Henry never a man to be thwarted could not refrain from his grumbling complaints.

Henry may have been away on progress but he made sure that a watch was kept on Anne and her correspondence. In the *Proceedings and Ordinances of the Privy Council of England*, it is noted that in July that 'William Sheffield, lately one of the retinue at Calais, was apprehended, for having said he had letters from the lady Anne of Cleves to the Duke of Norfolk, and was brought before the council and searched, when it was found that his letters were only from one Edward Bynings of Calais to Mrs. Howard, the old duchess of Norfolk's woman, to Mrs. Katharine Bassett, and Mrs. Sympson, the lady Anne of Cleve's women, which were but letters of friendship from private individuals;

yet he was committed for further examination'.[10] They found no evidence of wrongdoing on Anne's part and she would be grateful given the circumstances that followed.

Henry was devoted to his new queen but Katherine Howard was besotted with Thomas Culpeper and it was now her chequered past came to light. On 2 November 1541, Cranmer slipped Henry a letter at mass that told of her life in the Dowager Duchess of Norfolk's household. Mary Hall, who had worked at the Dowager's, had informed her brother John Lascelles who in turn told Cranmer of Katherine's behaviour with Francis Dereham and Henry Mannox. Cranmer interviewed Mary and was astounded by what he heard. When she tried to talk to Mannox about his behaviour he had apparently told her 'Hold thy peace, woman! I know her well enough. My designs are of a dishonest kind, and from the liberties the young lady has allowed me, I doubt not of being able to effect my purpose. She hath said to me that I shall have her maidenhead, though it be painful to her, not doubting but I will be good to her hereafter'.[11] Dereham had also been many times to the girl's dormitories and worse had spent time in Katherine's bed.

Henry would not believe his rose without a thorn had acted inappropriately but agreed to an investigation. He said 'he could not believe it to be true, and yet, the accusation having once been made, he could be satisfied till the certainty hereof was known; but he could not, in any wise, that in the inquisition any spark of scandal should arise against the Queen'.[12] From the testimony of witnesses including the men involved there was no doubt that Katherine had not been a virgin when she married the king. Mannox swore 'he never knew her carnally'[13] but admitted they had had a relationship. Dereham however 'hath had carnal knowledge of the Queen'.[14] Still this was before her marriage so for the time being Katherine was still safe.

Henry left Katherine at Hampton Court while he returned to London and left his councillors to her interrogation. Dereham in the meantime brought up the name of Thomas Culpeper in a bid to show his relationship with the queen had ended with her marriage and not continued on and that Culpeper had succeeded him in the queen's affections. This was explosive news and a search of his lodgings turned up a letter from the queen:

Master Culpeper,

I heartily recommend me unto you, praying you to send me word how that you do. It was showed me that you was sick, the which thing troubled me very much till such time that I hear from you praying you to send me word how that you do, for I never longed so much for a thing as I do to see you and to speak with you, the which I trust shall be shortly now. The which doth comfortly me very much when I think of it, and when I think again that you shall depart from me again it makes my heart to die to think what fortune I have that I cannot be always in your company. It my trust is always in you that you will be as you have promised me, and in that hope I trust upon still, praying you that you will come when my Lady Rochford is here for then I shall be best at leisure to be at your commandment...

yours as long as life endures,

Katheryn.[15]

Katherine's maid Jane Boleyn, wife of Anne Boleyn's brother George, who had testified against her husband and sister-in-law now admitted that Culpeper had been in the queen's private chamber and 'hath known the queen carnally considering all things that this deponent hath heard and seen between them'.[16] She believed they had committed adultery.

Katherine was moved to Syon Abbey, Middlesex under house arrest refusing to admit her relationship with Culpeper but she did confess her relationship with Mannox and Dereham in a letter to the king:

First at the flattering and fair persuasions of Manox being but a young girl (I) suffered him at sundry times to handle and touch the secret parts of my body which neither became me with honesty to permit nor him to require. Also Frauncis Dereham by many persuasions procured me to his vicious purpose and obtained first to lie upon my bed with his doublet and hose and after within the bed and finally he lay with me naked and used me in such sort as a man doth his wife many and sundry times but how often I know not and our company ended almost a year before the Kings majesty was married to my Lady Anne of Cleves and continued not past one quarter of a year or a little above. Now the whole truth being declared unto your majesty I most humble beseech the same to consider the subtle persuasions of young men and the ignorance and frailness of young women.[17]

She never would admit to her liaison with Culpeper. It made no difference. The evidence was damning enough and Culpeper and Dereham were executed at Tyburn on 10 December 1541 whilst Katherine awaited her fate. Jane Boleyn was incarcerated in the Tower and there too had to bide her time.

Henry returned to Hampton Court. Apparently Anne's only comment on her successor's fall from grace was 'She was too much of a child to deny herself any sweet thing she wanted'.[18] Anne knew she had had a lucky escape. She was at Richmond waiting for news or perhaps a summons to see the king but the only message she received was a request to return a ring Katherine had given her. The ring was 'only worth 3 gold cr. unless the stone, as is said, has some virtue against spasms'.[19] Chapuys reported that Anne 'greatly rejoiced at the event'[20] of Katherine's downfall but how he came about that conclusion we cannot tell.

The ambassador also debated her suitability as queen should the king consider taking her back but thought she was now not suitable due to her fondness of wine and 'indulging in other excesses'.[21] In the Spanish ambassador's eyes, she had gone from being dull to being over the top. Anne would never make a friend of Chapuys and it seemed as if she could not win, whatever her behaviour. Marillac had also complained at her attitude to the ending of her marriage – 'she is as joyous as ever, and wears new dresses every day; which argues either prudent dissimulation or stupid forgetfulness of what should so closely touch her heart'.[22] But once more rumours were circulating that Henry might still make Anne his queen and Marillac added to them by reporting 'As to whom the King will take, everyone thinks it will be the lady he has left, who has conducted herself very wisely in her affliction and is more beautiful than she was and more regretted and commiserated than Queen Catherine was in like case'.[23]

Jane Ratsey, one of Anne's ladies, was examined by the council for her slanderous conversation with another stated as Elizabeth but probably being Katherine Bassett. Ratsey had idly commented that 'God is working His own work to make the Lady Anne of Cleves queen again' to which Bassett replied 'it was impossible that so sweet a queen as the Lady Anne could be utterly put down'. Ratsey commented 'What a man the king is! How many wives will he have?' When interrogated Ratsey explained she had only said what she did on hearing of Katherine's downfall and 'was sorry for the change and knew not so much as she knows now'.[24]

The rumours were compounded by others reporting how close the king had grown to his 'sister'. Perhaps too close. In December amidst the investigation into Katherine's behaviour another investigation was ordered but this time it focused on whether Anne had given birth to a son of the king's. It is strange that Henry would have asked for the situation to be investigated if he had not slept with her but would Anne really have welcomed him to her bed given all that had happened between them, and would Henry have really have slept with his ex-queen when he was happy with Katherine at the time? He may also have just wanted the rumours quashed or to find out if Anne had had an illegitimate child by another man.

Henry felt 'it requisite to have it groundly [thoroughly] examined, and further ordered by your discretions, as the manner of the case requireth; to inquire diligently, whether the said Anne of Cleves hath indeed had any child or no, as it is bruited [reported], for his majesty hath been informed that it is so indeed, in which part his majesty imputeth a great defaut in her officers, for not advising his highness thereof, if it be true. Not doubting but your lordships will groundly examine the same, and finding out the truth of the whole matter, will advise his majesty thereof accordingly'.[25]

Members of Anne's household were interrogated including Dorothy Wingfield and Jane Ratsey again and those of the king's. Richard Taverner, a clerk of the signet office and Mrs Frances Lilgrave, Anne's lady and a court embroiderer 'were imprisoned three days ago for having said, since the Queen's misbehaviour was published, that the whole thing seemed a judgment of God, for the lady of Cleves was really the King's wife, and that though the rumour had been purposely spread that the King had had no connection with her, the contrary might be asserted, as she was known to have gone away from London in the family way, and had been confined last summer, - a rumour which has been widely circulated'.[26]

The council took the matter seriously and reported back to the king:

We examined, also, partly before dinner and partly after, a new matter, being a report that the lady Anne of Cleves should be delivered of a fair boy, and whose should it be but the king's majesty's? which is a most abominable slander, and for this time necessary to be met withal. This matter was told to Taverner of the Signet, more than a fortnigh ago, both by his mother-in-law (Lambert's wife, the goldsmith), and by Taverner's own wife, who

saith he heard it of Lilgrave's wife, and Lambert's wife heard it also
of the old lady Carew. Taverner kept it (concealed it), but they (the
women) with others have made it common matter of talk. Taverner
never revealed it till Sunday night, at which time, he told it to Dr.
Cox to be further declared if he thought good, who immediately
disclosed it to me the lord privy seal. We have committed Taverner
to the custody of me the bishop of Winchester; like wise Lambert's
wife (who seemeth to have been a dunce in it), to Mr. the chancellor
of the augmentations.[27]

The council completed their interviews. Anne was never interrogated and it was decided these were just malicious rumours. The mention of old Lady Carew gives reason to believe that Wymonde Carew, Anne's disgruntled servant, may have been behind them. What is extraordinary about the whole matter is that Henry thought it worth investigating. Other people certainly believed Anne had had at least one child by the king possibly two and there are some who claim they are Anne's descendants even today.

Anne's brother William had heard the news of Katherine Howard's fall and immediately thought to press for Anne's restoration. Olisleger was instructed to write to Cranmer and the Lord Privy Seal for their support. Ambassador Harst dutifully passed on the letters but neither man wanted to become involved. Cranmer was well aware that Cromwell had died because of his involvement in the Cleves marriage. He was not about to support a situation that could lead to his own downfall. Harst tried to see the king back in November but was not granted an audience. When he finally addressed the council on 14 December:

After declaring his master's thanks for the King's liberality to his
sister, prayed them [to find] means to reconcile the marriage and
restore her to the estate of queen. They answered, on the King's
behalf, that the lady should be graciously entertained and her estate

rather increased than diminished, but the separation had been made for such just cause that he prayed the Duke never to make such a request. The ambassador asking to have this repeated, Winchester, with every appearance of anger, said that the King would never take back the said lady and that what was done was founded upon great reason, whatever the world might allege. The ambassador dared not reply, for fear that they might take occasion to treat her worse...[28]

The decision was final. Henry would never take back Anne. Some historians believe that Anne held out hope of remarriage and was disappointed but given she had a new lease of life as the king's sister and had felt the fear and terror of having displeased the king and kept her head, it is hardly likely she would risk everything again even if her brother believed it in her best interest.

Katherine Howard

Chapter Seven

The King's Sister
1542–1546

Anne and Henry had exchanged New Year's gifts but seldom saw each other. In January Henry heard of a book that had been published in France *The Remonstrance of Anne of Cleves* which depicted Anne as a wronged sorrowful woman. It spoke to Henry – 'Let him then take pity of her scalding tears and show compassion for her sorrow. Let him give place to her great and perfect love, and grant that by his kindness she may live content. Let him retain this his most humble servant, this his creature, who was only born for him; and let him not use such cruelty as that she, without having done him any ill or offence, should be repudiated and divorced, and so rendered the most miserable and unfortunate wife in the whole world'.[1]

And even had Anne contemplating suicide 'the law forbids her doing violence to herself, to send her soul back to heaven whence it came; yet she cannot live in the world without dying daily in deaths far more cruel than words can describe'.[2] It roused great sympathy for her but Henry wanted it suppressed. Written by John of Luxembourg, son of the Count of Brienne, it was printed in France late 1541. By the time Henry saw it, it had been widely distributed but William Paget, once Anne's secretary, was sent over to Francis I to stop its circulation. The wily French king pretended he knew nothing of the book but agreed to suppress it adding 'the lady Anne is yet of age to bear children, and albeit the wind hath been contrary it may fortune to turn'.[3] Francis I was now allied to Cleves through William's marriage to Jeanne d'Albret, his niece and would support Anne's remarriage to Henry if it came about.

Marillac, the French ambassador, had advised Karl Harst to

wait until Katherine Howard's fate was decided before again pressing the king to marry Anne. There was European interest now as to whether Cleves would once more be allied with England and he gave the Queen of Navarre, mother of Jeanne d'Albret, a good report of Anne:

> *All her affairs could never make her utter a word by which one might suppose that she was discontented; nay, she has always said she wished nothing but what pleased the King her lord; thus showing an example of rare patience in dissembling passions common to everyone, which could only come of singular grace of God and a heart resolved to accept what could not be remedied. She has behaved, with her household, so wisely that those who visit her marvel at such great virtue, others who hear of it are loud in her praise, and all regret her much more than they did the late Queen Katharine.*[4]

The council's decision had been final but Harst had letters from German princes supporting a remarriage. After talking to Marillac it was decided to wait for Francis I's permission before he presented them to the king. Charles V wrote to Chapuys that he had heard 'some talk of Henry taking back Anne of Cleves, which must, if possible, be prevented'.[5] But with shifting political alliances, permission was not given and once again the subject was dropped – this time for good.

Katherine Howard's fate however had been decided. On 10 February 1542 Katherine was taken by barge from Syon Abbey to the Tower of London, passing under London Bridge where the heads of Dereham and Culpeper looked down on her. The poor girl was terrified and had to be assisted to the Tower where 'she weeps, cries and torments herself miserably without ceasing'.[6] On the evening of 12 February, she was told to make ready her soul and prepare for death. She then asked for the block to be brought to her so that she would know how to position herself.

The next morning she was led out 'The Queen was so weak that she could hardly speak, but confessed in few words that she had merited a hundred deaths for so offending the King who had so graciously treated her'.[7] Her execution was swift and her body was taken to the Chapel of St Peter ad Vincula for burial. Jane Boleyn followed her to the block. Although she had been declared insane at the beginning of the year, the king saw her as implicit in the downfall of his queen. Being mad she could not stand trial but Henry passed a law which meant the insane could be executed for high treason. The unfortunate woman was buried close to her mistress.

Henry spent the day hunting at Waltham and then returned to Whitehall for three days of Lenten feasts. He was in a much better mood receiving the court ladies 'with much gaiety'.[8] Anne was ill in March with tertian fever and he sent his good wishes and his doctors but that was all. He had no need to see his ex-wife especially when she was sick. Anne was suffering ill health on and off and it may have been through the strain of ongoing renegotiations of her marriage. At one point Dr Butts prepared a remedy for her of chamomile, hyssop and linseed 'to mollify, resolve, comfort and cease pain of cold and windy causes'.[9] Her relationship with her receiver Wymonde Carew had improved enough for him to be really concerned for her. She was troubled that she had no response to her enquiries about Henry's health and wished for some cramp rings. Cramp rings were known as a cure for many illnesses including epilepsy and convulsions and blessed by the King on Good Friday. Carew wrote to John Gates of the privy chamber to ask his brother-in-law Anthony Denny to see if Henry would contact her telling him he felt 'not best at ease'[10] at Anne's discomfort. What her actual illness was then we don't know.

But the news that was to come in the summer would not make her life any easier. Mary of Hungary wrote to Chapuys:

Francis is daily increasing his army on the Luxemburg frontier, and the infantry force which his ministers have raised on the side of Cleves and Gueldres. We have remonstrated through the Imperial ambassador and asked if he mean to observe the truce of Nice. But he only says that the assembly on the frontier of Cleves is for defence, not invasion, as long as we do not give him occasion, for he hears Henry is about to make alliance with the Emperor and the Count de Roculx is meditating an attack on some French towns. He has also sent a gentleman to give us notice that he intends sending his own officers to St. Pol to administer justice, and collect the revenue a formal demonstration that he means war. We have therefore ordered the immediate levy of 25,000 foot and 4,000 horse, with which force, and that of the King of England's subjects in those parts, we hope to defend our frontiers. We have discovered treacherous dealings here and there to surprise towns and fortresses.[11]

Anne worried over her brother William who supported by Francis I declared war on Charles V in July after a long running dispute over Guelders. Whilst Francis' men attacked Luxembourg and Perpignan, William's troops under the command of Maarten van Rossum, the 'Guelders Atilla'[12] travelled through the Brabant region 'sacking, destroying, and setting fire to the houses and fields of the poor peasantry'[13] before laying siege to Antwerp. There were many English merchants in the city, many who had welcomed Anne on her journey to England, and Henry was asked for his help to ensure their safety but he had no wish to involve himself with a war against the Holy Roman Emperor. In fact he was secretly negotiating with Charles V against France and would sign a treaty with him the following year. The siege failed and the merchants of Antwerp were safe. William's troops continued to battle against the emperor's forces and in November there was a report that Juliers 'had been ravaged and desolated with fire and plunder by the Imperial forces'.[14]

Anne had a quiet Christmas while she waited for news of

her family but was moved from her melancholy in March when Henry sent a message he would like her company at Hampton Court. She stayed for three days but Chapuys reported the king saw her only once and 'paid little attention to her'.[15] Back at Richmond she heard of Charles V's proclamation against her brother 'the duke of Clèves has not only allied himself with the enemies of the Holy Empire and Christian Republic, but has also so accustomed himself and his ministers to the manners and ways of those enemies, that he cannot speak one word of truth... What other proof does Germany require of the Duke's bad faith, and hostile intentions, than his refutation of the truce, and his notorious alliance [with the French], in order to prevent any resistance against the Turk, the ally and confederate of the latter, to keep the whole of Germany in trouble and contention, and thereby impede the peace and welfare of Christendom?'[16] She knew her brother would cling on to his right to Guelders until the last but the war was not going well for him and she could only wonder where it would lead.

Henry had granted Anne permission to see the Princess Mary and she welcomed her to Richmond in June. Anne was twenty-eight, Mary twenty-seven and the women had much to talk about it. It was a lovely break from the news of war in the Low Countries and her solitude at the palace. Mary was so pleased with her stay that she gave presents of money to Anne's officers and servants.

Had they heard the rumours that Henry was set to marry again and to the sister of one of Mary's women? Henry had his eye on Katherine Parr from at least February when he first gifted her pleats and sleeves and ordered gowns for her in the Italian fashion though she was a married woman. Katherine was the daughter of Sir Thomas Parr, a descendant of Edward III. She had been widowed at the age of sixteen but two years later was proposed to by Lord Latimer of Snape Castle in Yorkshire. She often attended court with her husband but by 1543 it was well known that her husband was unwell and had not long to live. After her husband died she hoped to marry Sir Thomas Seymour, brother of Henry's third wife, but it was not to be. Henry had him sent as an ambassador to Brussels. His rival was now out of the way.

Katherine had no real desire to become the next queen of England but Henry courted her as a wounded soul 'sad, pensive and sighing'.[17]

To become Henry's sixth wife was even more dangerous than it had been. The Act of Attainder that condemned Katherine Howard also stated that 'an unchaste woman marrying the King shall be guilty of high treason'.[18] It was no secret that Henry would take no more chances with his wives and if they proved unfaithful they would be executed. Katherine Parr had been married twice before so was not exactly 'a pure and chaste maid' but her family were loyal to the crown and had served past and present kings. Henry had had enough of foreign princesses and the changing alliances they brought with them. He was determined to marry an English lady.

On 12 July 1543 the thirty-one year old Katherine Parr became the aging Henry's sixth wife. Henry by now had grown 'very stout and daily growing heavier, he seems very old and grey... three of the biggest men to be found could get inside his doublet'.[19] The Princess Mary was invited to the wedding along with her siblings, not so Anne. It was a quiet wedding held in the Queen's Closet at Hampton Court Palace with Stephen Gardiner, Bishop of Winchester, officiating. Only twenty of their closest family and friends attended.

Katherine would prove to be the soothing balm to Henry's temper taking as her motto 'To be useful in all I do'. But she was also clever and astute improving Henry's relationship with his children and becoming a supporter of the 'new religion'. Wriothesley wrote 'the king's majesty was married on Thursday last to my lady Latimer, a woman, in my judgement, for virtue, wisdom and gentleness most meet for his highness; and sure I am his majesty had never a wife more agreeable to his heart than she is. The Lord grant them long life and much joy together'.[20]

What Anne thought of this new marriage we do not truly know but Chapuys reported she was upset:

> *Indeed, as far as I can hear from an authentic quarter, the said Dame would greatly prefer giving up everything that she has and living with her mother in Germany, to remaining any longer in England, treated as she is, and humiliated and hurt as she has lately been at the King marrying this last lady, who is by no means so handsome as she herself is, besides which there is no hope of her having children, considering that she has been twice a widow and has borne none from either of her deceased husbands.*[21]

But it must be remembered that Chapuys was the Emperor's man and no friend to Anne. As Starkey has suggested 'he was eager to bring about a final rupture between England and Cleves and eager, too, to get Anne out of the way'.[22]

Henry personally rode out to Richmond to dine with Anne and tell her of his marriage as he had done after his wedding to Katherine Howard. By now Anne had settled into her own way of life. If Henry had wanted her back she would have remarried him for the prestige and alliance it gave her family and Cleves but he was no longer an attractive proposition. Neither was returning to war devastated Cleves where she would be seen as the rejected wife of a king rather than the wealthy 'sister' she had become.

Plague in the city meant the court moved away from London during the summer. Anne must have moved too perhaps to Bletchingley or Hever to escape the disease. Hans Holbein was not as fortunate. The court artist who had painted Anne's portrait and that of her sister succumbed to an illness sometime before November of that year. Thomas Cawarden was still keeper of Bletchingley and when Anne visited, he and his wife Elizabeth decamped to Hextalls nearby. But Cawarden, a keen reformer, also spent much of his time at court as a Gentleman of the Privy Chamber and it was here he heard that his name had been mentioned in relation to heresy. Four men had just been tried under the Act of Six Articles and sentenced to die. One of Katherine's Parr servants, Fulke, had heard that others had been mentioned at their trial and papers were on their way to Stephen Gardiner, Bishop of Winchester and member of the Privy Council, that named names. Cawarden intercepted the missive and it was rumoured kidnapped the messenger and had him held at the Earl of Bedford's lodgings. Sure enough his name was mentioned along with many of the king's personal servants and their wives. But Henry was appalled there had been a private inquiry, not one authorised by himself, and all those mentioned were pardoned.

In August Anne heard with horror that Charles V had laid siege to Duren, the capital of Juliers, with 36,000 foot and 8000 horse. Six hundred houses were burnt to the ground with almost every other house damaged by a barrage of shot. On the fifth assault Duren fell with 'the garrison, and most of the inhabitants, being put to the sword'.[23] The bad news did not end there. Anne's mother died at the end of August and was buried in the Carthusian charterhouse at Wesel near Dusseldorf. It was said that she died from the grief of losing Juliers and the devastation of its people 'raging and in a manner out of her wits (as it is reported) for spite and anger of the loss of her country'.[24]

William had no choice now but to surrender and in September he met with Charles V to sign the Treaty of Venlo. He gave up Guelders and Zutphen but Charles allowed him to keep Juliers – what was left of it. To cement the alliance William divorced the French Jeanne d'Albret which must have been a relief to the young girl who had been dragged to the altar. 'On Easter Day the young Princess D'Albret made a public declaration in a chapel in the palace of Plessy, where the King was present, to the effect that she had never wished to contract marriage with M. de Cleves; and she swore this by the body of God of which she had that day partaken, and by the holy gospels'[25] and plans were now made for William to marry Maria of Austria, the Emperor's niece.

Life settled down for Anne and the next two years were peaceful. Henry happy in his last marriage made sure she was well looked after and granted her extra finances when needed. He had paid one William Lok, mercer, Thomas Hungate, havener, to the late Queen Jane, and William Fulwoode, merchant tailor, for themselves and others named in a warrant of 24 June, 328*l*. 12*s*. 'for necessaries bought for the lady Anne of Cleves'.[26] When the Duke of Prussia sent him gifts of falcons he also thanked him for the white osprey that had been sent to Anne. Mary visited her again at Richmond and she sent the king's daughter a gift of silk.

But Henry was far from ready to hang up his boots, and set off to France at the end of September 1544 leaving Katherine Parr as regent. Henry had always yearned for a glorious victory over his arch enemy but apart from the capture of Tournai in 1513 it had never really happened. Henry knew he was getting no younger. His waist was now 54 inches and his chest measured 57 inches. He was so large he needed help to move around the palace let alone climb on a horse. He was in no state to lead an army but he was not to be thwarted.

In July 40,000 men of the king's army were mustered at Calais. Some to take Montreuil, the others, commanded by the sixty-year-old Duke of Suffolk, to lay siege to Boulogne. Henry joined his lifelong friend to watch the destruction of the French town but it was no easy victory. Boulogne had two sections, high and low. The lower section fell with ease but the high section and its castle took a draining amount of time, weakening the men and resulting in many casualties. It was decided to dig under Boulogne's stone foundations to breach the castle and on

13 September the town surrendered to Henry's delight and his troops' relief.

Henry returned to England at the end of September 1544 leaving the Dukes of Suffolk and Norfolk, who had abandoned the siege on Montreuil, to defend Boulogne. With a large French force arriving in the area, the English army withdrew to Calais against the king's wishes, leaving only 4,000 men for its defence. Henry was furious but there was nothing he could do.

The political situation in 1545 saw Henry at odds with France, the Holy Roman Empire and Scotland. England was on the defensive. The Earl of Hertford was sent to Scotland with an army should French troops attempt to cross the Scottish borders, 30,000 men were mustered to protect the south coast and the Lord Admiral was at sea with 12,000 men should an invasion be attempted. Henry once more turned to the Schmalkaldic League. John Frederick of Saxony, Anne's brother-in-law, would have nothing to do with Henry who he referred to as a 'crazy man' but its other leader Philip of Hesse was more amenable to discussion. Ambassadors were sent but with John Frederick absolutely refusing to enter into an alliance, their talks came to nothing.

Stephen Gardiner wrote:

We are at war with France and Scotland, we have enmity with the bishop of Rome; we have no assured friendship here with the empror and we have received from the landgrave, chief captain of the Protestants, such displeasure that he has cause to think us angry with him... Our war is noisome to our realm and to all our merchants that traffic through the Narrow Seas... We are in a world where reason and learning prevail not...[27]

But there would be no invasion and England would eventually feel a sense of peace. At home at least Henry had found that with Katherine Parr and he did not forget Anne. In December 1545 the king's payments including wages to Andrew Staill, Richard Bloundell and Thomas Charde, gentlemen to the Lady Anne of Cleves, Cornelius Zifridus, her doctor of physic, Thomas Carew, John Bekynsall, a gentleman usher and John Barnardyne, an Italian. Wymonde Carew had left her service by now and was serving Queen Katherine as her treasurer.

The following year it was reported that 'Lady Anne of Cleves has been for some time at Court, well treated'[28] but her sojourn to court caused more rumours about her relationship with the king and whether she had had his children at home and abroad. In May John Dymock 'being in the house of Walter Henricks in Cronenborch in the state of Dordrecht, about eleven o'clock midday, there came in the bailiff of Dordrecht, with Doctor Nicholas, physician, and the bailiff asked him and his host to dinner. They went, and about half an hour later were joined by the procuréur général and three others. The procureur asked Dymock not to take ill what should be said to him in confidence, and first one Van Henluyden asked if it were true that the King had taken again Lady Anne of Cleves and had two children by her. Dymock answered that they in England knew no more than he had heard here, — it was a matter between God and the King. Dymock was then asked the reason why the King put away the Lady of Cleves, and replied that that was asking too much of him, but it was not without reason, and he thought that men ought to be content with what the King did in his own country'.[29]

The truth was that Henry was ailing and that he had no strength for a relationship with his wife let alone Anne. A fever had struck him down for three weeks in March. His leg was troubling him but he rallied and made plans for a summer progress although all those that saw him thought he was an ill man.

Anne was back and forth to court attending on the queen. Whereas she had never formed a friendship with Katherine Howard, the amiable, likeable Katherine Parr included her in court life. The princesses Mary and Elizabeth were also welcome due to Katherine's insistence and she became a loving stepmother to them. Henry was surrounded by his family but Katherine only narrowly escaped his ire in March 1546. The Imperial ambassador Van der Delft wrote 'I am confused and apprehensive to have to inform your Majesty that there are rumours here of a new Queen, although I do not know why, or how true it may (be)'.[30] Though some thought Henry might have his eye on the Duchess of Suffolk, the late Charles Brandon's wife.

The queen was known for her reformist views and she had tried to express herself to the king 'frankly to debate with the king touching religion, and therein flatly to discover herself; oftentimes wishing, exhorting, and persuading the king, that as he had, to the glory of God, and his eternal fame, begun a good and a godly work in banishing that monstrous idol of Rome, so he would thoroughly perfect and finish the same, cleansing and purging his church of England clean from the dregs thereof, wherein as yet remained great superstition'.[31]

But Henry was not impressed and, spurred on by Gardiner, a devout Catholic and Bishop of Winchester, he gave assent for her arrest. Katherine found out what was happening when she saw a copy of the bill of articles against her. She knew now that she was in danger and close to losing her head as other queen's had done. Taking the initiative she sought Henry out who 'began of himself, contrary to his manner before accustomed, to enter into talk of religion, seeming as it were desirous to be resolved by the queen, of certain doubts which he propounded'.[32] She knew this was a trap too easily to fall into and instead passively told her husband 'Since, therefore, that God hath appointed such a natural difference between man and woman, and your Majesty being so excellent in gifts and ornaments of wisdom, and I a silly poor woman, so much inferior in all respects of nature unto you, how then cometh it now to pass that your Majesty, in such diffuse causes of religion, will seem to require my judgment?

which when I have uttered and said what I can, yet must I, and will I, refer my judgment in this, and in all other cases, to your Majesty's wisdom, as my only anchor, supreme head and governor here in earth, next under God, to lean unto'.[33] It was all about Henry – his will was her will. She would do nothing to go against him and had only been debating religion with him as way to take his mind off the pain in his leg. Henry replied 'Is it even so, sweetheart? And tended your arguments to no worse end? Then perfect friends we are now again, as ever at any time heretofore'.[34] Henry had been appeased but Wriothesley had already been instructed to arrest her the following day.

When Katherine was out walking with the king in his privy garden, he approached her with forty guards. But the king attacked him shouting 'Knave! Arrant knave, beast! And fool!' The he commanded Wriotheseley 'presently to avaunt out of his presence. Which words, although they were uttered somewhat low, yet were they so vehemently whispered out by the king, that the queen did easily, with her ladies aforesaid, overhear them; which had been not a little to her comfort, if she had known at that time the whole cause of his coming, as perfectly as after she knew it'.[35] It was a public display that showed to the world that Katherine was safe. Anne must have heard of the queen's jeopardy and been relieved that like herself, she had survived the wrath of the king.

Anne sent congratulations to her brother William who married the fifteen-year-old Maria of Austria at Regensburg in July. Her gift to them both was a pair of greyhounds and two horses. Maria or Mary was the daughter of Ferdinand I, brother of the Charles V. Unlike his first marriage, this one would prove to be happy and provide the couple with seven children.

All was well between the king and his sixth wife by August when Henry summoned Anne to attend the reception for the Admiral of France, Claude d'Annebault, after England had finally made peace with the treaty of Ardes in June. Hall was impressed with the celebrations 'to tell you of the costly banqueting houses, that were built, and of the great banquets, the most costly masks, the liberal huntings that were shown to him, you would much marvel and scant believe'.[36] Henry was hardly able to keep up with the revels, leaning heavily on Cranmer, and Anne noticed the extra attention the queen paid to him. Henry was unwell and unknown to Anne this would be the last time she would be in his presence at court.

The Execution of Lady Jane Grey

Chapter Eight

The King is Dead! Long Live the King!
1547–1553

Henry's health took a turn for the worst in December 1546 and he wrote his will on the 30th. He saw in the New Year but as January progressed it was apparent the king was failing. As he approached his demise those around him wanted to tell him his end was near but to talk of the king's death was treason. It was Anthony Denny, Chief Gentleman of the Privy Chamber, who finally told his master 'You are not like to live'[1] and urged him to make his peace with God, asking if he wished for a priest. Henry replied 'I will first take a little sleep and then, as I feel myself, I will advise upon the matter'.[2] Archbishop Cranmer was sent for anyway to undertake the last rites at Henry's bedside. Henry was unable to speak now but when Cranmer asked for a sign he trusted in God the king 'holding him with his hand, did wring his hand in his as hard as he could'.[3] In the morning of 28th January 1547, this once strong and proud King died in his fifty-fifth year, with his close confidant, Cranmer, by his side.

The king's death was kept a secret and his body stayed in his chamber for three days while political wheels turned. His son Edward would be pronounced King but someone would be needed to guide his reign. Henry had made provision for a regency council but Edward Seymour, the brother of Henry's wife Jane and Edward's uncle, saw himself as fulfilling the role of Lord Protector to assist the young prince. Seymour spent the time between Henry's death and Edward's proclamation rallying his supporters to him.

Seymour had already taken Edward from Hertford Castle to where the Princess Elizabeth was staying at Enfield to ensure that the new king was under his control. It was rumoured that when they were told of their father's demise, brother and sister clung to each crying and sobbing for the man who had featured so largely in their lives. On 31st January, Wriothesley announced to parliament that Henry VIII was dead. On the same day Edward was proclaimed king with Edward Seymour by his side.

Edward instructed his council 'If ye have not already advertised my lady Anne of Cleves of king Henry's death, it shall be well done if ye send some express person for the same'.[4] Anne was no longer the king's sister but a widow and she could only wonder what her life would be like now.

King Henry's body was transported by a gilded chariot pulled by eight horses to St George's Chapel in Windsor. The roads from Westminster to Windsor had been prepared to allow the four-mile long procession to pass. It stopped at Syon Abbey for the night where it is said that Henry's coffin burst open and dogs licked at his remains. Once the coffin was repaired, Henry continued on to his final resting place alongside the wife he had loved the most, the wife that had given him his only legitimate son, Jane Seymour. King Henry was buried on 16 February in St George's Chapel at Windsor Castle with none of his family present apart from Katherine Parr who watched from the privacy of the Queen's Closet. It took sixteen strong yeomen to carry his coffin to its resting place. After masses were said and Henry's coat of arms, helmet, shield and sword were placed reverentially on the altar, the service was ended with the proclamation 'The King is dead! Long live the King!'

Edward was crowned at Westminster Abbey on 20th February 1547. Cranmer told the waiting congregation that there was no need to anoint the new king because he was already God's anointed 'elected by God, the King was accountable only to God'.[5] Edward was crowned three times with St Edward's crown, the imperial crown and a crown made especially for the young boy. He was handed the orb and sceptre, St Edward's staff and spurs and allowed each of the nobility to come forward and kiss his left cheek. England had its new king.

But this new boy king who had thought of Anne and that she should be told of his father's death would be no friend to her. Whereas Anne had built a relationship with Mary and Elizabeth, she had rarely seen Edward as cosseted as he was. Katherine Parr had moved to Chelsea and resumed her infatuation with Thomas Seymour, the Lord Protector's younger brother. Seymour wanted to marry her but was wary of the new king's reaction coming so soon after his father's death. He asked John Fowler, a gentleman of the privy chamber, to find out his thoughts. Edward suggested first that he marry Anne of Cleves but then thought Mary might be a better option and might give her a chance to 'change her opinions'.[6] Seymour managed eventually to get Edward's blessing for his marriage to Katherine and they were wed, some said with indecent haste, around April or May.

Anne had no intention of marrying anyone although members of the Privy Council thought it would be the best answer to her financial difficulties. In April Anne sent her officers to inform them that she had a yearly deficit of £120. During the old king's reign he had supported her and made up for any shortfall in her income. Due to Henry's depleted coffers he had instigated a policy where English coin was debased – the amount of gold and silver in coins was reduced and replaced with cheaper metals such as copper thus leading to rising inflation. It led to Henry being called 'Old Coppernose' as the silver wore off his nose revealing copper beneath it. Coin was devalued and Anne was struggling. The council agreed to make up her income as per her agreement with Henry but they also had an idea of what she could do with her properties to aid her finances. In December 1546, Bletchingley had been granted to its keeper and also Edward's Master of the Revels, Thomas Cawarden, on the event of Anne's death. The council now informed Anne that she should rent Bletchingley to him and in return receive one of Kent's oldest houses, Penshurst Place, built in 1341 and surrounded by deer parks, where Henry VIII had often hunted.

> *Madam, after due commendacions, wheras amonges other thing*
> *declard here oon your behalf by Sir John Guldford, knight, your*
> *Graces chamberlain, the same hath required an estate to be made*
> *unto you of the use of the kings Majesties house at Penshurst,*
> *the game and wood within the parke, in like mannour and forme*
> *as ye have presently at Blechinglegh, likeas we consydre that the*
> *commoditie of the sayd house of Penshurst shallbe mete for your*
> *purpose in respect of the nerenes of the same to Heyvour, and that*
> *forbearing nowe the commoditie of the house, game and woodes at*
> *Blechinglegh aforsayd, the rest of your revenues there shall stande*
> *you in no other stede and pleasor but for the certeyn rent of the*
> *same; we have thought good, in respect of the determinacion which*
> *we know to have been in the kings majestie, our late sovereign lorde*
> *decessed, to plante Sir Thomas Cawarden, knight, Gentleman of*
> *his Hieghnes Pryvie Chambre, in those parties when your Grace*
> *shuld receive other recompence, by theis to require your Grace to*
> *be content to make surrender unto him of all your title and interest*
> *in Blechinglegh for the mannour and thappurtenances, paying*
> *the yerely rent of xxxiiij (34) poundes xv (15) shillings and twos*
> *pennes sterling, with each assuraunce to be made unto him of*
> *the same as by the lerned counsaill of your Grace and him shalbe*
> *thought convenient, wherein your Grace shall for the tyme have*
> *such a tenante as will see your revenue assuredlye and honestly*
> *answered...*[7]

Anne did not want to give up Bletchingley nor take on Penshurst.
Her brother William sent his ambassador Heresbach over to help
her and he had an audience with the king on 11 April and then
spent four days with Anne at Hever. We don't know what help
he was as Anne reluctantly made Bletchingley over to Cawarden
for a yearly rent but he was rewarded with eighty gold crowns
for his assistance.

As well as trouble at home Anne was appalled to hear the current news from Europe. On 24 April 1547 the Battle of Mühlberg ended Charles V's war against the Schmalkaldic League. Her sister's husband John Frederick of Saxony who had commanded the league's troops was arrested and condemned to death. Her sister Sybilla had bravely played her part and organised the defence of Wittenburg but it was a lost cause. However it was reported that the Elector of Saxony took it very calmly:

The Elector, soon after his being taken prisoner, gave a fine instance of that constancy and sweetness of disposition which could not be overcome by the severest reverses. Charles, immediately after the battle, besieged Wittenberg; in which town Sybilla of Cleves, Frederic's wife, with their children, had hoped to be safe, and which for a while defied the utmost efforts of the imperialists. To terrify the place into a surrender, the Emperor condemned John Frederick to death; trusting that his wife, Sybilla, would purchase his life by the delivery of the town. When informed of the sentence, he had just sat down to his favourite game of chess, and looking up he calmly observed, 'This blow is levelled not against me, but against Wittenberg and my poor wife. Would that Sybilla could bear such news as well as I can! What is the loss or gain of a few days to a worn-out old man? To me the sentence has no terrors! Come, Ernest,' said he, then cheerfully turning to the Duke of Brunswick, his antagonist at chess and his fellow-prisoner, 'come, for all this we shall not lose our game'.[8]

On 19 May John Frederick signed the Capitulation of Wittenberg to save himself and his wife, ceding his rule to Maurice of Saxony and his death sentence was reduced to life imprisonment. Sybilla rode out to the Imperial camp and entreated Charles V to allow her husband to live quietly with her in Saxony but the emperor refused. Anne petitioned King Edward to seek John Frederick's release as did her sister. The boy king supported their request by sending an ambassador to speak on the duke's behalf but John Frederick would remain incarcerated until 1552.

In 1548 Anne lost her favourite palace of Richmond as well as her lands and properties in Ham and Petersham. She personally went to court to complain to the now Lord Protector, Edward Seymour.

Madam de Cleves arrived here a short time ago, the reason of her coming being, as I am informed, to speak to the Protector on certain complaints as to her treatment in money matters, and especially as regards the recompense for the house at Richmond, which has been taken away from her and prepared for the King. I understand that a favourable reply has been given to her.[9]

It was a huge blow. After being sent to Richmond against her will, she had come to love the palace and spent most of her time there. But in June Anne had no choice but to officially give Richmond back to the crown. Edward was appalled at the state of disrepair the palace had fallen into and had to spend £1000 on immediate repairs. Anne had little money in past years and it was obvious she had not spent anything on its upkeep. Edward granted her the King's Manor at Dartford in exchange.

In the second year of his reign in consideration of the surrendry of lands in Surrey, granted to the lady Anne of Cleves, the repudiated wife of Henry VIII, sundry premises in Dartford, lately belonging to the Priory, there late in the occupation of Sir Richard Longe, knight, and the amount of £30 ys. yd. reserved as a rent for the same; and also the manor of Dartford with its appurtenances, belonging to the late priory; a certain tenement in Overy, late in the tenure of Thomas Maythin ; "his park called Washmede in Dartford," in tenure of Robert Dove ; the site of the late monastery or priory of Dartford, together with the houses, buildings, gardens, and *orchards, belonging to the said priory, with all waters, fisheries, wears, courtleet, views of frank pledge, liberties, warren, etc., with other premises therein mentioned to the late priory belonging to him in Dart ford, to hold for the term of her natural life, or so long as she should reside within the realm, at the yearly rent of £18 16s. 1 1\2d.*[10]

Anne had stayed at Dartford Priory on her first entrance to London back in 1540. Not long after Henry had this building part demolished including 'breaking uppe of toumes and tomb stones in the church'[11] and a manor house constructed in its place. Although it was not a palace it had over a hundred rooms but it too was in disrepair and it would be five years until Anne could use it as a home. Anne spent most of her time between houses. She still owned Hever and often stayed at Bletchingley and Thomas Cawarden's house in Blackfriars. Her brother continued to worry over her income and treatment and sent his ambassadors to Edward over the coming years to make sure she was looked after. Anne once again considered returning home.

Katherine Parr died on 5 September at Sudeley Castle, six days after giving birth to Seymour's daughter, Mary. Seymour had always been jealous of his brother's rise to power and sought advancement for himself but his actions led him to ruin. Not only had he tried to court the Princess Elizabeth but on the night of 16 January 1549, he broke into Hampton Court Palace making for Edward's apartments with a pistol in his hand. As he made his way to the king's chamber one of his loyal dogs raised the alarm and was shot by Seymour. It was never made clear what his true intentions were although he protested he was just making sure Edward was safe. He was arrested and accused of thirty-three charges of treason.

When Thomas Seymour was executed on 20 March 1549 Anne wrote to her brother William 'God knows what will happen next'.[12] The reign of the new king was not running smoothly and she was greatly troubled. Her finances were one of her main concerns. She told William 'everything is so costly here in this country that I do not know how I can run my house'.[13] In December 1549 Renard reported that 'The Duke of Cleves has sent to the King of England Drossart de Montjoye and Dr. Croeser to obtain the payment of arrears of the pension that has here been accorded and granted to his sister [i.e. Anne of Cleves]. The Duke has also sent me a letter asking me to favour them in their mission. It is thought there will be no difficulty'.[14] When ambassador Cruser arrived again from Cleves in 1551 it was rumoured that she might return with him but as Renard reported again 'the councillors came to an agreement, as the ambassador himself told me. According to his account, they have behaved reasonably enough; and it seems the Archbishop of Canterbury shewed the said lady favour'.[15] With assurances she would be looked after and Cranmer's support Anne decided to stay.

However her troubles were not over. Edward now required she give up her manor and lands at Bisham, Berkshire and in November 1552 it was noted 'The Lady Ann of Cleves is dissatisfied'.[16] She wrote a letter to the Princess Mary about her situation early in January 1553.

Madam, After my most hearty commendations to your grace, being very desirous to hear of your prosperous health, wherein I very much rejoice, it may please you to be advertised that it hath pleased the king's majesty to have in exchange my manor and lands of Bisham, in the county of Berkshire, granting me in recompense the house of Westropp, in Suffolk, with the two parks and certain manors thereunto adjoining; notwithstanding, if it had been his highness' pleasure, I was well contented to have continued without exchange. After which grant, for mine own assurance in that behalf, I have travailed, to my great cost and charge, almost this twelve months; it hath passed the king's majesty's bill, signed, and the privy seal being now, as I am informed, stayed at the great seal, for that you, madam, be minded to have the same, not knowing, as I suppose, of the said grant. I have also received at this Michaelmas last past part of the rent of the aforesaid manors. Considering the premises, and for the amity which hath always been between us (of which I most heartily desire the continuance), that it may please you therefore to ascertain me by your letters or otherwise, as it shall stand with your pleasure. And thus, good madam, I commit you unto the ever-living God, to have you in merciful keeping... Your assured loving friend to her little power to command, Anna, the dowghter of Cleves.[17]

She had at least been offered Westhorpe Hall in Suffolk, the previous residence of Charles Brandon, Duke of Suffolk. It had been a grand house in its day but since its reversion to the crown in 1541 little had been done with it and there is no record that Anne ever stayed there. Anne was raging at yet a further loss to her properties but here would be no approaching the king to discuss the situation.

King Edward VI had been ill for most of the year suffering with his chest. He died on 6 July 1553 probably of tuberculosis. In an act that contravened his father's wishes, Edward wrote a new Device for the Succession excluding his sisters and instead left the rule of the realm 'to the Lady Frances's heirs male, for lack of (if she have any) such issue (before my death) to the Lady Janes heirs males'.[18] Frances was the daughter of Mary Tudor, Henry VIII's younger sister and Charles Brandon but she had no male heirs only daughters. Edward then amended the device from 'Lady Janes heirs males' to 'Lady Jane and her heirs males'. Lady Jane Grey was Frances' eldest daughter and Edward was determined that the succession of England would stay within the Suffolk line.

Why did Edward rule out Mary and Elizabeth? It seems that with the taint of illegitimacy hanging over his sisters Edward felt that his cousins' bloodline was purer. Parliament had declared both the princesses illegitimate in 1536 as both of their mother's marriages to the king were deemed null and void. He wrote

> ...that the ladie Jane, the ladye Katherine, and the ladie Marye, daughters of our entirely beloved cosen the ladie Fraunces, nowe wife to our lovinge cosene and faithfull counsellor Henry duke of Suffolke, and the ladie Margarete, daughter of our late cosene the ladie Elleonore deceased, sister of the saide ladie Frauncis, and the late wife of our welbeloved cosen Henry earle of Cumberland, being very nigh of our whole bloude, of the parte of our father's side, and being naturall-borne here within the realme, and have ben also very honorably brought upe and exercised in good and godly learninge, and other noble vertues, so as ther is greate truste and hope to be had in them that they be and shalbe very well inclined to the advancement and settyng forth of our comon welth.[19]

During his brief reign Edward had a fractious relationship with Mary who refused his orders not to hear Catholic mass and openly flaunted her religious beliefs. The young king was adamant that England would not mend its break with Rome and felt that Mary would return the nation to Catholicism. However there was no real reason to pass over Elizabeth apart from his belief she was only half-blood.

Lady Jane Grey, of 'small features and a well-made nose, the mouth flexible and the lips red. The eyebrows are arched and darker than her hair, which is nearly red'[20] was declared queen on 10 July to a stunned crowd uncertain of what this meant to England's future. One small boy, Gilbert Potter, found his voice and loudly announced that the Princess Mary had more right to the throne – echoing the sentiment of the crowd – for which he was arrested.

Mary herself was seething. She was now thirty-seven and her life had not been a happy one. She had always upheld that her mother had been Henry's one true wife and she was not about to see a young girl take the throne that she knew to be hers. On the same day as Jane was crowned a letter was delivered to the Privy Council in which Mary asserted her rights.

My lords, we greet you well and have received sure advertisement that our dearest brother the King and late sovereign lord is departed to God. Marry, which news, how they be woeful unto our hearts, He wholly knoweth to whose will and pleasure we must and do humbly submit us and our will.

But in this lamentable case, that is to wit now after his departure and death, concerning the Crown and governance of this Realm of England with the title of France and all things thereunto belonging, what has been provided by act of Parliament and the testament and last will of our death father – beside other circumstances advancing our right – the Realm know and all the world knoweth. The rolls and records appear by authority of the king our said father and the king our said brother and the subjects of this Realm, as we verily trust that there is no good true subject that is or can or will pretend to be ignorant hereof. And of our part, as God shall aid and strengthen us, we have ourselves caused and shall cause our right and title in this behalf to be published and proclaimed accordingly.

And, albeit this manner being so weighty, the manner seemeth strange that our said brother, dying upon Thursday at night last past, we hitherto had no knowledge from you thereof. Yet we considered your wisdoms and prudence to be such that having eftsoon among you debated, pondered, and well weighed this present case with our estate and your estate, the commonwealth, and all your honours, we shall and may conceive great hope and trust and much assurance in your loyalty and service, and that you will like noble men work the best.

Nevertheless, we are not ignorant of your consultations and provisions forcible, there with you assembled and prepared – by whom and to what end God and you know, and nature can but fear some evil. But be it that some consideration politic of some whatsoever reason hath hastily moved you thereto, yet doubt you not, my lords, we can take all these your doings in gracious part, being also right ready to remit and fully pardon the same freely, to eschew blood-shed and vengeance of those that can or will amend. Trusting also assuredly you will take and accept this grace and virtue in such good part as appeareth, and that we shall not be enforced to use the service of other our true subjects and friends which in this our just and rightful cause God, in whom our final affiance is, shall send us.

Wherefore, my lords, we require you and charge you, for that our allegiance which you owe to God and us, that, for your honour and the surety of your persons, you employ your selves and forthwith upon receipt hereof cause our right and title to the Crown and government of this realm to be proclaimed in our City of London and such other places as to your wisdoms shall seem good and as to this case appertaineth, not failing hereof, as our very trust is in you. And this letter signed with our hand shall be your sufficient warrant.[21]

She was residing at the well-fortified Framlingham Castle and rallying her supporters to her cause. She did not have long to wait. On 19 July Mary was proclaimed Queen of England to resounding cheers. Bonfires were lit and church bells rang out across London. Poor Lady Jane, known as the nine-day queen was moved to the Tower. Her mother desperately sought an audience with Mary to plead for her and other members of their family who had been involved in her assent but Mary was advised to show no leniency and Jane would be charged with treason.

In August four Spanish ambassadors sent a missive to Charles V:

Last Sunday a solemn predication was held at St. Paul's by a doctor who has long been associated with the Bishop of Winchester. Several members of the Queen's Council were present, and the yeomen of the guard, for the protection of the said preacher, who discoursed pertinently on the holy sacrament. The sermon was well received, without murmurs or interruptions. Mass is sung habitually at Court; not one mass only, but six or seven every day, and the Councillors assist. My Ladies of deves (sic) and Elizabeth have not been present yet.[22]

Mary's rule immediately instigated changes in religious worship. After the Protestant focus of Edward's rule, Mary insisted on a return to the old Catholic ways and she insisted with a vengeance. At Mary's first parliament she had all religious legislation passed in her brother Edward's reign repealed and the validity of her mother's marriage was reinstated – finally making her legitimate once more. As many nobles and gentry realised the danger they would face as Protestants in a changing England they fled across the water to Strasbourg, Basle, Zurich, Frankfurt and Geneva.

The Duchess of Suffolk was one who left. Mary's government would later try to stop the duchess and other exiles from receiving revenue from their lands. William Cecil, who would feature prominently in Elizabeth's reign, opposed the bill, informally named after the duchess. He echoed many councillors thoughts when he said 'although with danger to myself, I spoke my opinion freely and brought upon me some ill will thereby, but it is better to serve God than man'.[23] Many were caught between their religious beliefs and the threat to their safety. But Anne was more than happy to follow Mary's example. After all her mother had raised her as a Catholic and she would be content to attend mass unlike the Princess Elizabeth.

Mary, who Anne had remained friends with throughout her life in England, now took the throne. Anne was included in the celebrations. The day before her coronation Mary travelled from the Tower to Westminster in a chariot

of cloth of tissue drawen by sixe horses, all trapped with the like cloth of tissue. She sate in a gowne of purple velvet furred with powdered ermine, having on her head a caule of cloth of tinsell, beset with pearle and stone, and above the same upon her head, a round circlet of gold beset so richly with precious stones, that the value thereof was inestimable, the same caule and circlet being so masste and ponderous, that she was faine to beare up her head with her hand, and the canapy was borne over her chariot. Before her rode a number of gentlemen and knights, then judges, then doctors, then bishops, then lords, then the councell: after whome followed the knights of the Bathe, thirteene in number, in their robes, the bishop of Winchester lord Chancelor, and the marquesse of Winchester lorde high treasurer, next came the duke of norffolke, and after him the Earle of Oxforde, who bare the sword before her, the maior of London in a gowne of crimosin velvet bare the scepter of gold, &c. after the Queenes chariot, sir Edward Hastings led her horse in is hand: then came an other chariot, having a covering all of cloth of silver all white, and sixe horses trapped with the like, therin sate the lady Elizabeth and the lady Anne of Cleve, then Ladies and Gentlewomen riding on horses trapped with red velvet, and their gownes and kirtles likewise of red velvet: after them followed two other chariots covered with red sattin, and the horses betrapped with the same, and certaine gentlewomen betweene every of the saide chariots riding in crimosin sattin, their horses betrapped with the same, the number of the gentlewomen so riding were 46 besides them in the chariots.[24]

Mary was crowned on 1 October 1553 and at the coronation banquet afterwards Anne sat with Elizabeth at the top table with their new queen. It would be Anne's last public appearance but after the trials and troubles of Edward's reign she would now be in favour and have a far better relationship with the reigning monarch – or so she hoped. Amongst the many letters of congratulation was one from Mary, Duchess of Cleves and Juliers, Anne's sister-in-law.

Anne was welcome at court and visited Mary in October. Discussions about who Mary should marry were rife and Anne suggested Ferdinand II, Archduke of Austria. Ferdinand was Charles V's nephew and also related to her brother William through marriage. A match between them would again link Cleves to England but Anne was to be disappointed. Mary had already set her sights on Philip of Spain. Supporters of this match saw Anne as a threat and the Spanish ambassador Renard was unhappy with Anne's interference. He also reported:

> My Lady [Anne] of Cleves is taking steps to get her marriage to the late King Henry VIII declared legitimate, so that she may enjoy the dowry, treatment and prerogatives of a Queen Dowager of England, and also continue to enjoy her dowry even if absent from England. We hear that the case will be adjourned till later; when more urgent and important affairs have been settled and decided.[25]

Again it was rumoured that Anne wanted to go home but whereas her situation in Edward's reign had been an uncomfortable one, her future was now looking brighter. Anne was no threat but neither would she be granted her wish to be made queen dowager. Her relationship with Mary was such that she could approach her with suggestions but the new queen had much more pressing issues to deal with than Anne's concerns.

Edward VI

Chapter Nine

Queen Mary's Reign
1554–1556

Although Anne may have had Mary's ear she was not so favoured as to deter suspicion. The people of England had welcomed Mary to the throne but when rumours spread that Mary wished to marry a Spanish husband, discontent surfaced. Sir Thomas Wyatt along with the Duke of Suffolk, Sir James Croft and members of the Carew family plotted uprisings in different parts of the country. The plan was to take control of the Welsh marches, the midlands and the south-west and then march to London but with lack of support only Wyatt carried out the rebellion in the south-east.

On 26th January 1554, Wyatt took Rochester in Kent and demanded that Mary should be imprisoned in the Tower of London before he began to march towards London. If Mary was to be placed in the Tower then it followed that Elizabeth would replace her as queen and surely Elizabeth had some part in organising such a rebellion that would put her on the throne. Mary suspected her sister but also Anne of aiding her.

Mary was still determined to marry Philip of Spain, the Emperor's son, and Renard, the Imperial ambassador who had filled Chapuys' position at court, informed Charles V that the king of France would do anything to stop the marriage, even if it meant war 'because he has promised the Duke of Cleves, at the lady Elizabeth's request, thus to revenge himself for Henry VIII's repudiation of his sister'.[1] Both Elizabeth and Anne were seen as being in league with France. It was Anne who had suggested a marriage to Ferdinand after all which proved her loyalty to her brother certainly but not the king of France. He also reported 'The Queen, moreover, told me that the Lady (Anne) of Cleves was of the plot and intrigued with the Duke of Cleves to obtain help for Elizabeth'.[2]

Anne was also suspected of her involvement by her association with Thomas Cawarden. Cawarden had been arrested at the outbreak of the rebellion by Lord William Howard, James Skinner and John Skinner. After being questioned he was allowed to return to Bletchingley, which he was renting from Anne, and told to prepare his servants to march at an hour's notice to intercept the rebels. Bletchingley had a vast armoury and it seems Cawarden could not be trusted to use it for the queen's sake. Lord William Howard sent instructions to the sheriff Sir Thomas Saunders to 'immediately take, carry and convey away from the house of Sir Thomas Cawarden, knight, all such harness, weapons, guns, munitions of war, and horses...'[3] He was arrested again and after a spell at Skinner's house in Reigate was taken to London and finally placed under house arrest in Blackfriars.

Wyatt first made for London Bridge where Mary's forces turned the rebels away with cannon shot. Wyatt's army made for Kingston-upon-Thames in Surrey where the bridge across the river had been destroyed to stop his men from crossing the murky waters. After repairing it they marched on to London.

Mary gave a rallying speech at London's Guildhall. She told the crowds of people who had gathered to see her:

I am your Queen, to whom at my coronation, when I was wedded to the realm and laws of the same (the spousal ring whereof I have on my finger, which never hitherto was, not hereafter shall be, left off), you promised your allegiance and obedience to me.... And I say to you, on the word of a Prince, I cannot tell how naturally the mother loveth the child, for I was never the mother of any; but certainly, if a Prince and Governor may as naturally and earnestly love her subjects as the mother doth love the child, then assure yourselves that I, being your lady and mistress, do as earnestly and tenderly love and favour you. And I, thus loving you, cannot but think that ye as heartily and faithfully love me; and then I doubt not but we shall give these rebels a short and speedy overthrow.[4]

The rebellion was halted at Ludgate. Wyatt surrendered and was imprisoned in the Tower where he was tortured in the hope that he might incriminate Elizabeth.

Renard reported on 12 February 1554:

The Queen of England summoned me this morning and informed me that the Council had issued orders for Courtenay's arrest and imprisonment in the Tower, because Wyatt, without having been tortured, accused him and several others, such as Pickering and Poignz, of being of the conspiracy. Pickering escaped arrest by flight into France, where he is said to have joined Carew... The Council has sent two of the Queen's physicians to visit the Lady Elizabeth and find out whether she is still unwell or only pretending, and whom she has in her house; and if she is not ill the Admiral, Hastings and Cornwallis are to arrest and bring her in to the Tower. The Queen, moreover, told me that the Lady (Anne) of Cleves was of the plot and intrigued with the Duke of Cleves to obtain help for Elizabeth: matters in which the King of France was the prime mover. In order to smooth them over the French ambassador had audience to-day, though I do not yet know exactly what he said. The Queen says that God has miraculously permitted all this to come out and furnished her with means to put a stop to it by punishing the guilty authors in time, for otherwise heresy would have found its way back to the kingdom, she would have been robbed of her state and England subjected to the will of the French. So she is now absolutely determined to have strict justice done and make herself strong against further eventualities.[5]

On the same day that Renard wrote his despatch Lady Jane Grey was executed. Dressed in black and carrying her prayer book, she was led out to the green at the Tower were she spoke her final words.

> Good people, I am come hither to die, and by a law I am condemned to the same; the fact indeed against the Queen's Highness was unlawful and the consenting thereunto by me: but touching the procurement and desire thereof by me or on my behalf, I do wash my hands thereof in innocency before the face of God and the face of you good Christian people this day…
>
> I pray you all good Christian people to bear me witness that I die a true Christian woman and that I do look to be saved by no other mean, but only by the mercy of God, in the merits of the blood of his only son Jesus Christ. I confess when I did know the word of God I neglected the same and loved myself and the world, and therefore this plague or punishment is happily and worthily [deservedly] happened unto me for my sins. I thank God of his goodness that he has given me a time and respite to repent.
>
> Now good people, I pray you to assist me with your prayers. Now good people, while I am alive, I pray you to assist me with your prayers.[6]

Jane then recited Psalm 51, the Misere, in English 'Have mercy upon me O God, after they great goodness: according to the multitude of thy mercies, do away mine offences'. She took off her gown, headdress and collar and asked the executioner to despatch her quickly. Placing a blindfold over her eyes, Jane panicked as she tried to feel for the block. She was helped to find it and praying 'Lord, into thy hands I commend my spirit' she was swiftly killed with one blow.

On 16 March 1554 Elizabeth was charged with prior knowledge of the Wyatt rebellion but no further action was taken against Anne. Elizabeth was interrogated but they had no proof of her involvement. Sir Thomas Wyatt was executed but as he stood on the scaffold he exonerated Elizabeth saying,

'And whereas it is said and whistled abroad that I should accuse my lady Elizabeth's grace and my lord Courtenay; it is not so, good people. For I assure you neither they nor any other now in yonder hold or durance was privy of my rising or commotion before I began. As I have declared no less to the queen's council. And this is most true'.[7] Elizabeth was released but placed under house arrest. Both the princess and Anne had had a lucky escape. Nothing could be proved against Cawarden either and he returned to his official duties in March. Anne had not even been interrogated which seems surprising given Mary's distrust. But neither was she now in favour.

In April 1554 the ambassador Cruser was sent to inform Anne of the deaths of Sybilla and John Frederick. Sybilla had died at the end of February and John at the beginning of March. They were buried in the church of St Peter and St Paul at Weimar. Their eldest sons John Frederick II and John William inherited their father's lands when he was imprisoned but after his death they divided his remaining lands between them. The electorship of Saxony had been lost through the Capitulation of Wittenberg and John Frederick II would unsuccessfully spend the rest of his life trying to regain his father's title.

Mary was married on 25 July 1554 at Winchester Cathedral with Gardiner, the Bishop of Winchester, officiating. Mary was delighted to finally have a husband but the twenty-six-year-old Philip had little interest in Mary. His adviser Ruy Gomez reported that 'it will take a great God to drink this cup [but]… the king realises that the marriage was concluded for no fleshly consideration, but in order to remedy the disorder of this kingdom and to preserve the Low Countries'.[8] For Philip their match was purely political. Anne was not invited to the celebrations but she wrote the queen a note:

To the Queen's Majesty. After my humble commendations unto your majesty, with thanks for your loving favour showed to me in my last suit, and praying of your highness your loving continuance, it may please your highness to understand that I am informed of your grace's return to London again, and being desirous to do my duty to see your majesty and the king, if it may so stand with your highness' pleasure, and that I may know when and where I shall wait on your majesty and his. Wishing you both much joy and felicity, with increase of children to God's glory, and to the preservation of your prosperous estates, long to continue with honour in all godly virtue. From my poor house at Hever, the 4th of August.[9]

Mary returned to Westminster on 18 August before travelling to Hampton Court for the rest of the summer. Anne was not called to court as she had hoped in her letter and had to content herself with her needlework and an interest in cookery. In November it was reported Mary was pregnant but there would never be any children born to the couple. In the same month The Revival of the Heresy Acts was passed and read:

For the eschewing and avoiding of errors and heresies, which of late have risen, grown, and much increased within this realm, for that the ordinaries have wanted authority to proceed against those that were infected therewith: be it therefore ordained and enacted by authority of this present Parliament, that the statute made in the fifth year of the reign of King Richard II, concerning the arresting and apprehension of erroneous and heretical preachers, and one other statute made in the second year of the reign of King Henry IV, concerning the repressing of heresies and punishment of heretics, and also one other statute made in the second year of the reign of King Henry V, concerning the suppression of heresy and Lollardy, and every article, branch, and sentence contained in the same three several Acts, and every of them, shall from the twentieth day of January next coming be revived, and be in full force, strength, and effect to all intents, constructions, and purposes for ever.[10]

Mary wanted heretics to be punished with the full force of the law. She would earn the title 'Bloody Mary' for her persecution of Protestants throughout her reign with the deaths of over 280 men and women. She was devout and fervent in her belief. Those who did not follow her lead would suffer.

Thankfully Anne towed the religious line, never giving Mary any other cause to doubt her but she was saddened at not being asked to attend court. Her money troubles plagued her and she was by now having trouble with Thomas Cawarden who in December was three months late with his rent. She was staying at Hever and wanted the money so that she could travel to Penshurst Place for Christmas 'for I have a fair home and would fane be going before the holyday'.[11] Cawarden was angry with Anne for not spending any money on the upkeep of Bletchingley and may have been withholding her rent but Anne was in no position to provide financial assistance.

Anne still stayed at Bletchingley on occasion but she had also upset him when her staff had cut down trees for firewood and built new, and as he thought, useless outbuildings. He complained:

I gave her Grace wood for dispendinge in the house sythen her first comynge thether, of greate Oke, beache and Asshe by fowere, five, syx and seven score lodes at a time. And at hallowtyde laste, I gave them at there requeste ageanste her Graces comynge thether, syx hundred lode of wood or there aboutes by there owne reporte, which before the having thereof, theye sought by waye of requeste. After I had given them the seide lodes of wood, they seide it was there owne and that they myghte by present patente take it where and when they wolde and that I might nor oughte not denye them. And in myne absens her Officers did commence the making of coles and felled doune myne woodes by the grounde for the same, also fayre Okes, Asshes and Beches beinge good tymber wood (which they never presumed nor the lyke before this tyme) made to the number of

40 lodes and also besides a great deale which yet remanithe uncoled. Also where I did appoynte and delyver at her requeste sufficiente tymber for the necassarie reparinge of the house, they ithout myne consente and knoleage did fell a greate meanye of tymber trees and thereof made fower new houses of tymber and borde where none was before, which cannot be justified by the lawe. Also with my seide wooddes did furnesshe a commune bruhouse and also a vittelynge house in the contreye not without a great number of lodes and that of no worse wood than is before resyted.[12]

Back in May 1554 George Throckmorton was appointed by the Privy Council to govern Anne's household and it was reported that Anne was 'verye desirous to have (him) in the same rowme'.[13] One member of her household Florence de Diaceto was ambassador Olisleger's nephew. In December 1554 he was petitioning the Queen Mary for 'losses sustained in Wyatt's commotion' and for a licence to import 4000 tons of French wine.[14] He had been in Henry VIII's service receiving payments from him up until 1546 and was sent by Edward VI to the king of Denmark. It is uncertain what he was doing for Mary as a 'small time envoy and agent'[15] whilst in Anne's household but something went wrong in 1555. Wotton wrote:

Understands that Florence de Diaceto (nephew to the Chancellor of Cleves), born in Antwerp of Florentine parentage, who had a pension in England, but since her Majesty's accession having been in trouble and dismissed, has left England, and been seen in Paris by John Somer within these two days. As contrary to his former habit he would keep no company with Somer, Wotton has caused an eye to be had upon him, and been informed that he has been divers times with the Constable and with the whole Council, whereby it should seem he is here for no good intent. The person who had offered to supply her Majesty with secret information of the Court here, asks 50 crowns per mensem, which is more than Wotton dare give without knowing her Majesty's pleasure therein.[16]

Someone else who was in trouble was Archbishop Cranmer. Mary had never liked the man and blamed him for all that had gone wrong in her life. After all, it was he who had found the grounds for her mother's divorce from Henry VIII. He was responsible for not only paving the way for Anne Boleyn to take the throne but as she saw it he was also to blame for her father's break from the Church of Rome. Cranmer had been sentenced to death on 13 November 1553 but in 1554, he was moved to Bocardo prison in Oxford to await further trial for heresy.

On 21 March 1556, Cranmer was put to death. He had promised to renounce his Protestant faith and admit that Catholicism was the one true religion. At a service at the University Church in Oxford however, he used his final chance to speak to tell the world that the Pope was Christ's enemy and furthermore the Antichrist. He was dragged from the pulpit and tied to the stake. As the flames rose around him he placed his right hand – the hand that had signed away his true faith – into the fire. Cranmer would die a Protestant and martyr to the cause.

In the same month Anne heard that Thomas Cawarden was in trouble again. This time he was implicated in the Dudley plot to put Elizabeth on the throne and spent two months under house arrest at Blackfriars from May till July after which he returned to Bletchingley. Anne wanted to visit Blackfriars but had to ask for his help 'for her grace lacked money to buy the needful furniture, and she promised payment to Sir Thomas if he would make the purchases for her.'[17] Cawarden with whom she had such a tumultuous relationship supplied the house with all she could possibly want; gallons of wine, spices such as ginger, cinnamon, cloves and mace, mutton, capons, rabbits, wheat, firewood, coal, candles, pots, pans, kettles, skillets, ladles, skimmers, spits, trays and flaskets. Fresh fish like carp, pike and tench were also supplied 'for the trial of cookery'[18] so Anne could practise her culinary skills. Her household were not ideal guests and Cawarden found some of the items were 'broken, spoiled, and lost, and the rest remain at his house to his use, for which he asks no compensation'.[19]

One of her servants had been dismissed and now she heard that four others were in jeopardy. Count von Waldeck had spent time in her household but had been recalled to Cleves when Olisleger heard rumours he was trying to get Anne to make him her heir. The disgruntled count informed her brother William that she had servants about her who could not be trusted who came from Cleves and were his responsibility. Waldeck had particularly fallen out with Anne's cofferer Brockehouse who had put a reign on Anne's expenses and curtailed the expenditure of her household. William sent Karl Harst to ask Anne to discharge Brockehouse, his wife Gertrud – who was said to have driven Anne mad with her 'impostures and incantations'[20] – and Otho Wylik (the illegitimate son of Otto van Wylich, Lord of Huit and Grubbenvorst) and Thomas Chare, another member of her household, but she had refused. 'Every exertion has already been used, not a stone left unturned, to have them removed from her service, but in vain'.[21] Now her brother asked Queen Mary to become involved and in September the unfortunate servants were called before the council. Mary had had no contact with Anne for some time but she felt the need to intervene.

Brockehouse was told to 'departe from the house and family of the lady Anne of Cleve, and come never after in any of the same lady's houses, or where she shall for the tyme make her abode, ne do entromedle or busye himself in thadministracion of the government of her howseholde or other her affaires as her servant or officer'.[22] Brockehouse and his wife were ordered to leave England as was Otho Wylik. It is uncertain what happened to Chare.

William had also written to King Philip for his support and though he was absent from England he wrote from Ghent to say he 'approved of the measures relative to the Lady Anne of Cleves'.[23] Anne however did not approve and was unhappy to see her loyal servants go. She would need them beside her in the days to come.

Mary I

Chapter Ten

Final Days
1557

Anne moved to the manor at Chelsea in the spring of 1557. Henry VIII had exchanged lands here with Lord Sandys around 1536 so that he could build his own riverside mansion in what was then a pleasant, rural setting not too far from the city. The house had previously been home to the widowed Katherine Parr where she stayed with Thomas Seymour. The Princess Elizabeth too had lived here, both as a child and when under Katherine's care.

In April Sir Thomas Cornwallis was complaining Anne was being stubborn regarding the exchange of Westhorpe Hall. Mindful of losing yet more revenue, she was asking for the 'house and park in Gulford'.[1] Cornwallis wrote to William Cecil that he thought it would be hard to get for her. He blamed her cofferer Freston for 'her grace's disposition towards Westropp' and asked whether he would find out if Freston 'deals doubly'.[2]

Anne may have felt the pleasing air at Chelsea would help her. She had been unwell for some time but took to her bed with an undiagnosed illness on 12 July where she wrote her will. In it she made sure her household and those who had been loyal to her were rewarded. Each was to receive a year's wages and black cloth for their mourning clothes. She especially remembered her ladies 'for their great pains taken with us'.[3] She left Dorothy Wingfield and Dorothy Curzon £100 each and asked that Princess Elizabeth to take Curzon into her household. Susan Broughton was gifted £20 towards her marriage. Her laundress Elizabeth Eliot received £10 as did Mother Lovell who had looked after her during her sickness. Otho Wylik, the servant who had had to return to Cleves, was given £20.

She bequeathed to her brother a diamond and gold ring, his

wife received a ruby one. Diamond rings were also gifted to her sister Amelia, the Duchess of Suffolk and the Countess of Arundel. Count von Waldeck also received a ruby ring despite their disagreement. But her best jewel was left to Queen Mary and her second best to the Princess Elizabeth. There were gifts for her executors, Nicholas Heath, the Earl of Arundel, Sir Edmund Peckham and Sir Richard Preston and all who served her.

Anne even remembered those less fortunate with £4 being gifted to the poor of Richmond, Bletchingley, Hever and Dartford and £10 a piece to her alms-children for their education. Her final wish was that she was buried at the queen's 'will and pleasure' in the Catholic faith. (See Appendix Two for Strickland's version).

Anne died aged 41 on 16 July and after being embalmed laid in state for nearly three weeks. The Imperial ambassador later reported he had 'interrogated a widow who was in the service of the Duchess of Cleves till her death and was endowed by her. She told me that she had held the Duchess's hand when she was expiring. Everybody has nothing but good to say of the Duchess'.[4] Queen Mary wished her to be 'honourably buried according to the degree of such an estate'.[5] Her hearse travelled from Chelsea to Charing Cross from where the funeral procession left for Westminster Abbey.

After the priests, clerks, and monks with the crosses, came Bishop Bonner, with the Abbot of Westminster, followed by Sir Edmund Peckham, Sir Richard Preston (two of Anne's executors), the Lord Admiral, Lord Darcy, and numerous knights and esquires. Behind, there came the gentlemen of Anne's household, and the chariot containing her bier, on each side of which rode four heralds with white silken flags, as an emblem that she had lived and died a virgin, and twelve banners, some of arms, some of white taffeta, richly wrought with gold forming the rear. At Charing Cross, the procession was met by Anne's servants clad in mourning, and bearing an hundred lighted torches. At the Abbey door all the horsemen alighted, and the corpse, after Bishop Bonner had censed it, was carried in under a canopy of black velvet, and placed under the hearse. Dirge was then sung, and throughout the night, the bier, surrounded by burning tapers, was watched by the mourners.[6]

The following day Anne was buried. The diarist Henry Machyn wrote:

The iiij day of August was the masse of requiem for my lade prenses of Cleyff, and dowther to [William] duke of Cleyff; and ther my lord abbott of Westmynster mad a godly sermon as ever was mad, and [then] . . . the byshope of London song masse in ys myter; [and after] masse my lord byshope and my lord abbott mytered dyd [cense] the corsse; and afterward she was caried to her tomb, [where] she leys with a herse-cloth of gold, the wyche lyys [over her]; and ther alle her hed offesers brake ther stayffes, [and all] her hussears brake ther rodes, and all they cast them in-to her tombe; the wyche was covered her co[rps] with blake, and all the lordes and lades and knyghtes and gentyllmen and gentell-women dyd offer, and after masse agrett [dinner] at my lord (abbat's); and my lade of Wynchester was the cheyff [mourner,] and my lord admeroll and my lord Darce whent of ether syde of my lade of Wynchester, and so they whent in order to dinner.[7]

She was interred on the south side of the High Altar – the only one of Henry's wives to be buried at the abbey. It seems as though her monument with carvings of her initials, a crown, lions' heads and skull and crossed bones possibly started by Theodore Haveus of Cleves was never finished. A plain inscription on the back simply reads *Anne of Cleves Queen of England. Born 1515. Died 1557.*

Thomas Becon's *Pomander of Prayer* dedicated to Anne was reissued after her death (see Appendix Three). Anne's brother William ordered services to be held in her memory in every church in Cleves. Anne, a gentle soul, who escaped the most tyrannical Tudor king was largely forgotten. However a woman pretending to be Henry's fourth queen arrived at her nephew John Frederick's court at Coburg asking for protection. She was entertained for eighteen months until they realised she was mad.

Holinshed wrote that of Anne that she was 'a lady of right commendable regard, courteous, gentle, a good housekeeper and very bountiful to her servants'.[8] More than anything Anne was a strong woman and a survivor even though she sometimes saw herself as a stranger in a foreign land and she made a life for herself, a good life with friends and companions who loved her, despite being the unwanted wife of the King of England.

Appendix One

The Marriage Treaty

The treaty, which is here set forth textually, declares and provides:—

(1.) That a marriage has been concluded, by commissioners, between Henry VIII., king of England, &c., and lady Anne, sister of William duke of Juliers, &c., whose other sister, the lady Sibilla, John Frederic duke of Saxony, &c., has received in matrimony. (2.) That the duke of Juliers shall within two months, if he can obtain safe conduct, convey, at his own expense, the lady Anne his sister honourably to Calais. (3.) That there the King shall receive her, by his commissioners, and traduct her thence as soon as possible into his realm and there marry her publicly. (4) That if safe conduct cannot be obtained, which is very unlikely, the Duke shall send her, as soon as possible, to some sea-port and transport her thence to England with a suitable convoy of ships at his expense. (5.) That the Duke shall give with her a dote of 100,000 florins of gold, viz., 40,000 on the day of solemnisation of the marriage and the rest within a year after. (6.) That the King shall give the lady Anne, under his seal, a dower in lands worth yearly 20,000 golden florins of the Rhine, equal to 5,000 mks. sterling money of England, as long as she remains in England. And if, after the King's death, she have no children surviving and would rather return to her own country, she shall have a pension of 15,000 florins, payable half-yearly, for life, and her own dress and jewels; and it shall be at the choice of the King's heirs to pay the pension or redeem it with 150,000 florins. The sealed grant of this dower to be delivered to the Duke's commissioner on the day of the marriage and a true copy of it to be sent to the Duke ten days before her traduction. (7.) If the Duke die without lawful issue, and his duchy go therefore to the lady Sibilla, wife of John Frederic duke of Saxony, according to their marriage contract, and they in turn die without lawful issue, the succession shall go to the lady Anne. In the event of the succession going as aforesaid to the duke of Saxony a sum of 160,000 florins shall be paid within four years to the two sisters, the ladies Anne and Amelia, or their heirs; or if the succession come as aforesaid to the king of England he shall pay the 160,000 florins to the lady Amelia and her heirs. (8.) If the succession go to Saxony as aforesaid, and either of the two other sisters die without children, her share shall accrue to the surviving sister or her children. (9.) If the succession go to Saxony, then the lady Anne shall have, besides her dowry, the castles of Burdericum in Cleves with 2,000 florins a year, Casterium in Juliers with 2,000, and Benradum in Berg with 1,000, for life. (10.) That the duke of Juliers shall keep the King informed by letter of his proceedings for the transportation of the lady Anne, so that the King may thereby time his preparations for her reception. (11.) That the King and the said dukes of Saxony and Cleves shall confirm this treaty by letters patent under their hands and seals to be mutually delivered within six weeks from the date of this present, viz., by the King to the duke of Cleves and by the dukes to the King.

Appendix Two

The Last Will and Testament of Anne of Cleves

We, Anna, daughter of John, late duke of Cleves, and sister to the excellent prince William, now reigning duke of Cleves, Gulick (Juliers), and Barre, sick in body, but whole in mind and memory, thanks be to Almighty God, declare this to be our last will and testament: 1st, We give and bequeath our soul to the holy Trinity, and our body to be buried where it shall please God. 2dly, We most heartily pray our executors undernamed to be humble suitors for us and in our name, to the queen's most excellent majesty, that our debts may be truly contented and paid to every one of our creditors, and that they will see the same justly answered for our discharge. Beseeching also the queen's highness of her clemency to grant unto our executors the receipts of our land accustomed to be due at Michaelmas, towards the payment of our creditors. For that is not the moiety of our revenues, nor payable wholly at that time, and not able to answer the charge of our household, especially this year, the price of all cattle and other amt; (purchases) exceeding the old rate. 3dly, We earnestly require our said executors to be good lords and masters to all our poor servants, to whom we give and bequeath every one of them, being in our check-roll, as well to our officers as others, taking wages either from the queen's highness or from us, from the current month of July, one whole year's wages, also as much black cloth, at 13s. 4d. per yard, as will make them each a gown and hood, and to every one of our gentlemen waiters and gentlewomen accordingly. And to our yeomen, grooms, and children of our household, two yards each of black cloth, at 9s. the yard. Also to every one of the gentlewomen of our privy chamber, for their great pains taken with us, to Mrs. Wingfield, 100l; 20l. to Susan Broughton towards her marriage; to Dorothy Curzon, towards her marriage, 100l; to Mrs. Haymond, 20l. (To twelve other ladies, who seem in the like degree, she bequeath: various nuns, from 10l. to 16l. each.) To our laundress, Elizabeth Eliot, 10l, and to mother Lovell (this was the nurse of her sick room), for her attendance upon us in this time of this our sickness, 10l.

Item, we give and bequeath to every one of our gentlemen daily attendant on us, over and beside our former bequests (viz. wages and black cloth) 10l, that is to say, to Thomas Blackgrove, 10l, to John Wymbushe, 10l (eight gentlemen are enumerated); likewise to our yeomen and grooms, 11s. a-piece, and to all the children of our house 10s a-piece. And we give to the duke of Cleves, our brother, a ring of gold with a fair diamond, and to our sister, the duchess of Cleves, his wife, a ring, having therein a great rock of ruby, the ring being black enamelled. Also we give to our sister, the lady Emely, a ring of gold, having thereon a fair pointed diamond. And to the lady Katharine, duchess of Suffolk, a ring of gold, having a fair table diamond, somewhat long, and to the countess of Arundel a ring of gold, having a fair table diamond, with an H. and I. of gold set under the stone. Moreover, we give and bequeath to the lord Puget, lord privy seal, a ring of gold, having therein a three-cornered diamond, and to our cousin, the lord Waldeck, a ring of gold, having therein a fair great hollow ruby. Moreover, our mind and will is, that our plate, jewels, and robes, be sold with other of our goods and chattels, towards the payment of our debts, funerals, and legacies. And we do further bequeath to Dr. Symonds, our phisicon, towards his great pains, labours, and travails, taken oft-times with us, 20l; and to Alarde, our surgeon and servant, 4l; and to our servant John Guligh, over and above his wages, 10l; and to every one of our alms-children, towards their education, 10l a-piece, to be delivered according to the discretion of our executors. Also we will and bequeath to the poor of Richmond, Bletchingly, Hever, and Dartford, 4l to each parish, to be paid to the churchwardens at the present, and to be laid out by the advice of our servants thereabouts dwelling. And to our chaplains, sir Otho Rampello, and to sir Denis Thoms, either of them to pray for us, 5l and a black gown. And to our poor servant James Powell, 10l, and to Elya Turpin, our old laundress, to pray for us, 4l, and to our late servant, Otho Willicke, 20l; and our will and pleasure is, that our servants, sir Otho Rampello, Arnold Ringlebury, John Guligh, John Solenbrough, Derrick Pasman, Arnold Holgins, and George Hagalas being our countrymen, and minding to depart of this realm of England, shall have, towards their expenses, every one 10l. And we bequeath to Thomas Perce, our cofferer, to Thomas Hawe, our clerk-comptroller, and to Michael Apsley, clerk of our kitchen, for their pains with us taken sundry ways, over and beside their formal wages, 10l each. And our will and pleasure is, that our said cofferer, who hath disbursed much for us, for the maintenance of our estate and household, should be truly paid by our executors, likewise all other of our servants that hath disbursed any money for us at any time, if they have not been paid. The residue of all our goods, plate jewels, robes, cattle, and debts, not given or bequeathed, after our funeral debts and legacies, we give and bequeath to the right honourable Nicholas Heathe, archbishop of York, and lord chancellor of England, Henry earl of Arundel, sir Edmund Peckman, and sir Richard Preston, knights, whom we ordain and make executors of this our last will and testament. And. our most dearest and entirely beloved sovereign lady, queen Mary, we earnestly desire to be our overseer of our said last will, with most humble request to see the same performed as shall to her highness seem best for the health of our soul: and in token of the special trust and affiance which we have in her grace, we do give and bequeath to her most excellent majesty, for a remembrance, our best jewel, beseeching her highness that our poor servants may enjoy such small gifts and grants as we have made unto them, in consideration of their long service done unto us, being appointed to wait on us at the first erection of our household by her majesty's late father, of most famous memory, king Henry VIII., for that his said majesty said then unto us, 'that he would account our servants his own, and their service done to us as if done to himself.' Therefore We beseech the queen's majesty so to accept them in this time of their extreme need. Moreover, we give and bequeath to the lady Elizabeth's grace [afterwards queen Elizabeth] my second best jewel, with our hearty request to accept and take into her service one of our poor maids, named Dorothy Curzon. And we do likewise give and bequeath unto every one of our executors before named, towards their pains, viz. to the lord chancellor's grace, a fair bowl of gold with a cover; to the earl of Arundel, a maudlin standing cup of gold with a cover; to sir Edmund Peckham, a jug of gold with a cover, or else a crystal glass garnished with gold and set with stones; to sir Richard Preston, our best gilt bowl with a cover, or else that piece of gold plate which sir Edmund leaveth (if it be his pleasure), most heartily beseeching them to pray for us, and to see our body buried according to the queen's will and pleasure; and that we may have the suffrages of the holy church according to the catholic faith, wherein we end our life in this transitory world. These being witnesses, Thomas Perce, our cofferer, Thomas Hawe, our comptroller, John Symonds, doctor in physio, &c. ; also Dorothy Wingfield, widow, Susan Boughton, Dorothy Curzon, jantlewomen of our privy-chamber (bed chamber), with many others; and by me, Dionysius Thomow, chaplain and confessor to the same most noble lady Anna of Cleves.

Appendix Three

HONOURABLE AND VIRTUOUS LADY ANNE OF CLEVE, HER GRACE, SISTER TO THE HIGH AND MIGHTY PRINCE WILLIAM, DUKE OF CLEVE, &c., THOMAS BECON WISHETH THE FAVOUR OF GOD, LONG LIFE, AND CONTINUAL HEALTH.

Among many other godly and noble virtues, which God by his holy Spirit hath graffed in your grace's breast, most honourable lady, the fervent affection and continual desire of praying unto the Lord our God hath neither the last nor the least place in you. And as God hath wrought in you by the Holy Ghost this godly mind to call upon his holy name with diligent prayer, so likewise doth your grace stir up and con firm that spiritual motion with the exercise of daily prayer, lest that godly affection should be quenched, which the Holy Ghost hath kindled in your heart.

For your grace doth right well consider, that God delighteth in nothing more than in the invocation of his blessed name, and in the sacrifice of thanksgiving for his benefits. Where the name of God is diligently called upon, and most humble and hearty thanks given unto him for his fatherly and friendly gifts, there is his blessing, grace, and favour plenteous; there is the Holy Ghost present, there is a merry conscience; there all things prosper, there wanteth no good thing. Continue therefore, most honourable lady, as ye have godly begun, both you and all your faithful family, to call for the glorious name of the Lord our God with fervent prayer, and forget not to be thankful unto him for his benefits, wherewith above many other he hath richly endued your grace. So shall he be your loving Lord and gracious God, your favourable Father and strong shield. So shall he make your grace to prosper in all your doings, and bless you both with long life and much honour.

And that your grace may have at hand convenient prayers to

pray unto the Lord our God, I thought it good, considering your grace's manifold virtues, to give unto you this my Pomander of Prayer, wherein are briefly contained such godly prayers as are most meet in this our age to be used of all degrees and estates, most humbly beseech ing your grace to take in good part this my rude and bold enterprise, according to your accustomed gentleness. God, whose glory you heartily love, whose word you joyfully embrace, whose name you earnestly call upon, mought vouchsafe to preserve your grace in continual health and increase of honour! Amen.

Your grace's most humble and faithful orator, Thomas Becon.

References

Introduction

1. Tytler, *Tudor Queens and Princesses*
2. Hume, *The Wives of Henry the Eighth and the Parts They Played in History*
3. Burnet, *The History of the Reformation of the Church of England*
4. Strickland, *Lives of the Queens of England*

Chapter One: Early Days in Cleves 1516–1536

1. *Letters and Papers, Foreign and Domestic, Henry VIII*
2. Ibid.
3. Ibid.
4. Ibid.
5. Ibid.
6. McConica, *English Humanists*
7. Bietenholz, *Contemporaries of Erasmus: A Biographical Register of the Renaissance and Reformation*
8. McConica, *English Humanists*
9. Morris and Grueninger, *In the Footsteps of the Six Wives of Henry VIII*
10. Rank, *The Myth of the Birth of the Hero*
11. Ibid.

Chapter Two: The Search for a Bride 1537–1538

1. Palmer, *A Treatise on the Church of Christ*
2. Saaler, *Anne of Cleves*
3. Hall, *Hall's Chronicle: Containing the history of England*
4. Ibid.
5. *Letters and Papers, Foreign and Domestic, Henry VIII*
6. Wernham, *Before the Armada: The Emergence of the English Nation,*
7. *Letters and Papers, Foreign and Domestic, Henry VIII*

8. Cartwright, *Christina of Denmark Duchess of Milan and Lorraine*
9. *Letters and Papers, Foreign and Domestic, Henry VIII*
10. Lindsey, *Divorced Beheaded Survived,*
11. *Letters and Papers, Foreign and Domestic, Henry VIII*
12. Ibid.
13. Cartwright, *Christina of Denmark Duchess of Milan and Lorraine*
14. Koenigsberger, *Monarchies, States Generals and Parliaments: The Netherlands in the Fifteenth and Sixteenth Centuries*
15. *Letters and Papers, Foreign and Domestic, Henry VIII*
16. Ibid.
17. Ibid.
18. McEntegart, *Henry VIII, The League of Schmalkalden and the English Reformation*
19. Simpson, *The Autobiography of the Emperor Charles V*
20. Cartwright, *Christina of Denmark Duchess of Milan and Lorraine*
21. Ibid.
22. Ibid.
23. *Letters and Papers, Foreign and Domestic, Henry VIII*
24. Ibid.
25. Ibid.
26. Ibid.
27. Ibid.
28. Cartwright, *Christina of Denmark Duchess of Milan and Lorraine*
29. Ibid.

Chapter Three: Journey to England 1539

1. *Letters and Papers, Foreign and Domestic, Henry VIII*
2. Ibid.
3. Ibid.
4. Ibid.

5. Ibid.
6. Ibid.
7. Starkey, *Six Wives: The Queens of Henry VIII*
8. *Letters and Papers, Foreign and Domestic, Henry VIII*
9. Ibid.
10. Walker, Williston, *History of the Christian Church*
11. *Letters and Papers, Foreign and Domestic, Henry VIII*
12. Ibid.
13. Ibid.
14. Wilson, *Hans Holbein: Portrait of an Unknown Man*
15. Borman, *Thomas Cromwell*
16. Warnicke, *The Marrying of Anne of Cleves*
17. Weir, *The Six Wives of Henry VIII*
18. *Letters and Papers, Foreign and Domestic, Henry VIII*
19. Ibid.
20. Ibid.
21. Ruddock, *The Earliest Original English Seaman's Rutter*
22. *Letters and Papers, Foreign and Domestic, Henry VIII*
23. Saaler, *Anne of Cleves*
24. *Letters and Papers, Foreign and Domestic, Henry VIII*
25. Ibid.
26. Hall, *Hall's Chronicle: Containing the history of England*
27. *Letters and Papers, Foreign and Domestic, Henry VIII*
28. Warnicke, *The Marrying of Anne of Cleves*
29. Wilson, *Hans Holbein: Portrait of an Unknown Man*
30. Byrne, *The Lisle Letters*
31. *Letters and Papers, Foreign and Domestic, Henry VIII*
32. Ibid.
33. Holinshed, *Chronicles of England, Scotland and Ireland*
34. Starkey, *Six Wives: The Queens of Henry VIII*
35. *Letters and Papers, Foreign and Domestic, Henry VIII*
36. Saaler, *Anne of Cleves*
37. Byrne, *The Lisle Letters*

Chapter Four: The Marriage 1540

1. *Letters and Papers, Foreign and Domestic, Henry VIII*
2. Cox, *Miscellaneous Writings and Letters of Thomas Cranmer*
3. Morris and Grueninger, *In the Footsteps of the Six Wives of Henry VIII*
4. *Letters and Papers, Foreign and Domestic, Henry VIII*
5. Weir, *The Six Wives of Henry VIII*
6. Strype, *Ecclesiastical Memorials of Henry VIII, Edward VI and Mary,*
7. *Letters and Papers, Foreign and Domestic, Henry VIII*
8. Ibid.
9. Weir, *The Six Wives of Henry VIII*
10. Starkey, *Six Wives: The Queens of Henry VIII*
11. *Letters and Papers, Foreign and Domestic, Henry VIII*
12. Ibid.
13. Ibid.
14. Weir, *The Six Wives of Henry VIII*
15. Hall, *Hall's Chronicle: Containing the history of England*
16. Ibid.
17. *Letters and Papers, Foreign and Domestic, Henry VIII*
18. Ibid.
19. Ibid.
20. Ibid.
21. Ibid.
22. Weir, *The Six Wives of Henry VIII*
23. *Letters and Papers, Foreign and Domestic, Henry VIII*
24. Warnicke, *The Marrying of Anne of Cleves*
25. Starkey, *Six Wives: The Queens of Henry VIII*
26. *Letters and Papers, Foreign and Domestic, Henry VIII*
27. Ibid.
28. Ibid.
29. Strickland, *Lives of the Queens of England*
30. Weir, *The Six Wives of Henry VIII*
31. Norrington, *Anne of Cleves*

32. *Letters and Papers, Foreign and Domestic, Henry VIII*
33. Ibid.
34. Holinshed, *Chronicles of England, Scotland and Ireland*

Chapter Five: Cromwell's Downfall 1540

1. *Letters and Papers, Foreign and Domestic, Henry VIII*
2. Byrne, *The Lisle Letters*
3. Ibid.
4. Hamilton, *Wriotheseley's Chronicle*
5. Weir, *The Six Wives of Henry VIII*
6. Ibid.
7. Watkins, Sarah-Beth, *Lady Katherine Knollys*
8. *Letters and Papers, Foreign and Domestic, Henry VIII*
9. Ibid.
10. Ibid.
11. Weir, *The Six Wives of Henry VIII*
12. Lindsey, *Divorced Beheaded Survived*
13. *Letters and Papers, Foreign and Domestic, Henry VIII*
14. Ibid.
15. Ibid.
16. Warnicke, *The Marrying of Anne of Cleves*
17. Burnet, G., *The History of the Reformation of the Church of England*
18. Herbert, *The Life and Reign of King Henry VIII*
19. *Letters and Papers, Foreign and Domestic, Henry VIII*
20. Ibid.
21. Ibid.
22. Ibid.
23. Ibid.
24. Strickland, *Lives of the Queens of England*
25. *Letters and Papers, Foreign and Domestic, Henry VIII*
26. Ibid.
27. Ibid.
28. Strickland, *Lives of the Queens of England*

29. *Letters and Papers, Foreign and Domestic, Henry VIII*
30. Starkey, *Six Wives: The Queens of Henry VIII*
31. Denny, *Katherine Howard*
32. *Letters and Papers, Foreign and Domestic, Henry VIII*
33. Ibid.

Chapter Six: A New Queen Katherine 1541

1. *Letters and Papers, Foreign and Domestic, Henry VIII*
2. Ibid.
3. Ibid.
4. Ibid.
5. Ibid.
6. Hall, *Hall's Chronicle: Containing the history of England*
7. Freer, *The Life of Jeanne d'Albret, Queen of Navarre,*
8. Cartwright,
9. *Letters and Papers, Foreign and Domestic, Henry VIII*
10. Strickland, *Lives of the Queens of England*
11. Wilkinson, *Katherine Howard*
12. *Letters and Papers, Foreign and Domestic, Henry VIII*
13. Ibid.
14. Starkey, *Six Wives: The Queens of Henry VIII*
15. Wilkinson, *Katherine Howard*
16. Ibid.
17. *Letters and Papers, Foreign and Domestic, Henry VIII*
18. Denny, *Katherine Howard*
19. *Letters and Papers, Foreign and Domestic, Henry VIII*
20. Ibid.
21. Ibid.
22. Ibid.
23. Ibid.
24. Ibid.
25. Strickland, *Lives of the Queens of England*
26. *Letters and Papers, Foreign and Domestic, Henry VIII*
27. Ibid.

28. Ibid.

Chapter Seven: The King's Sister 1542–1546

1. Mackray, *The Remonstrance of Anne of Cleves*
2. Ibid.
3. *Letters and Papers, Foreign and Domestic, Henry VIII*
4. Ibid.
5. Ibid.
6. Weir, *The Six Wives of Henry VIII*
7. *Letters and Papers, Foreign and Domestic, Henry VIII*
8. Starkey, *Six Wives: The Queens of Henry VIII*
9. Saaler, *Anne of Cleves*
10. *Letters and Papers, Foreign and Domestic, Henry VIII*
11. Ibid.
12. Trio, *The Use and Abuse of Sacred Places in Late Medieval Towns*
13. *Letters and Papers, Foreign and Domestic, Henry VIII*
14. Warnicke, *The Marrying of Anne of Cleves*
15. *Letters and Papers, Foreign and Domestic, Henry VIII*
16. *CSP Spain*
17. Weir, *The Six Wives of Henry VIII*
18. *Letters and Papers, Foreign and Domestic, Henry VIII*
19. Hayward, *Dress at the Court of King Henry VIII*
20. *Letters and Papers, Foreign and Domestic, Henry VIII*
21. *CSP Spain*
22. Starkey, *Six Wives: The Queens of Henry VIII*
23. Carte, *A General History of England*
24. *Letters and Papers, Foreign and Domestic, Henry VIII*
25. *CSP Spain*
26. *Letters and Papers, Foreign and Domestic, Henry VIII*
27. Scarisbrick, *Henry VIII*
28. *Letters and Papers, Foreign and Domestic, Henry VIII*
29. Ibid.
30. Ibid.
31. Foxe, *Acts and Monuments*

32. Ibid.
33. Ibid.
34. Ibid.
35. Ibid.
36. Hall, *Hall's Chronicle: Containing the history of England*

Chapter Eight: The King is Dead! Long Live the King! 1547–1553

1. Foxe, *Acts and Monuments*
2. Ibid.
3. Ibid.
4. Strickland, *Lives of the Queens of England*
5. Starkey, *Elizabeth*
6. Skidmore, *Edward VI*
7. *Letters and Papers, Foreign and Domestic, Henry VIII*
8. *The British and Foreign Review*
9. *CSP Spain*
10. Dunkin, *The History and Antiquities of Dartford*
11. Morris and Grueninger, *In the Footsteps of the Six Wives of Henry VIII*
12. Saaler, *Anne of Cleves*
13. Ibid.
14. *CSP Spain*
15. Ibid.
16. *Calendar of State Papers, Domestic (Edward, Mary and Elizabeth)*
17. Everett Wood, *Letters of Royal and Illustrious Ladies of Great Britain*
18. *Calendar of State Papers, Domestic (Edward, Mary and Elizabeth)*
19. Ibid.
20. Hayward, *Dress at the Court of King Henry VIII*
21. Foxe, *Acts and Monuments*
22. *CSP Spain*
23. Alford, *Burghley*
24. Stow, *A Survey of London*

25. *CSP Spain*

Chapter Nine: Queen Mary's Reign 1554–1556

1. *CSP Spain*
2. Ibid.
3. Kempe, *The Loseley Manuscripts*
4. Foxe, *Acts and Monuments*
5. *CSP Spain*
6. Ives, *Lady Jane Grey*
7. Foxe, *Acts and Monuments*
8. Porter, *Mary Tudor*
9. Strickland, *Lives of the Queens of England*
10. Gee, *Documents Illustrative of English Church History*
11. Saaler, *Anne of Cleves*
12. Ibid.
13. Ibid.
14. *Calendar of State Papers, Domestic (Edward, Mary and Elizabeth)*
15. Allen, *Post and Courier Service in the Diplomacy of Early Modern Europe*
16. *Calendar of State Papers, Domestic (Edward, Mary and Elizabeth)*
17. Kempe, *The Loseley Manuscripts*
18. Ibid.
19. Strickland, *Lives of the Queens of England*
20. *Calendar of State Papers, Domestic (Edward, Mary and Elizabeth)*
21. Ibid.
22. Norrington, *Anne of Cleves*
23. *Calendar of State Papers, Domestic (Edward, Mary and Elizabeth)*

Chapter Ten: Final Days 1557

1. *Calendar of State Papers, Domestic (Edward, Mary and Elizabeth)*
2. Ibid.
3. Strickland, *Lives of the Queens of England*
4. CSP Spain
5. Saaler, *Anne of Cleves*

6. Strickland, *Lives of the Queens of England*
7. Nichols, *The Diary of Henry Machyn*
8. Holinshed, *Chronicles of England, Scotland and Ireland*

Select Bibliography

Ackroyd, Peter: *Tudors*, London, 2012

Acts of the Privy Council of England, Dasent, ed., London, 1890–1893

Alford, Stephen, *Burghley: William Cecil at the Court of Elizabeth I*, Connecticut, 2008

Allen, E J B., *Post and Courier Service in the Diplomacy of Early Modern Europe*, Berllin, 2012

Anglo, Sydney, *Spectacle Pageantry and Early Tudor Policy*, Oxford, 1969

Bacon, Francis, *The History of the Reign of King Henry VII and Selected Works*, Cambridge, 1998

Baldwin, David, *Henry VIII's Last Love: The Extraordinary Life of Katherine Willoughby, Lady-in-Waiting to the Tudors*, Stroud, 2015

Bernard, G.W., *The King's Reformation: Henry VIII and the Making of the English Church*, London, 2007

Bernard, G.W, *The Tudor Nobility*, Manchester, 1992

Bietenholz, *Contemporaries of Erasmus: A Biographical Register of the Renaissance and Reformation*, Toronto, 2003

Borman, Tracy, *Thomas Cromwell*, London, 2015

Burnet, G., (ed.), *The History of the Reformation of the Church of England*, Oxford, 1864

Calendar of State Papers, Domestic (Edward, Mary and Elizabeth)

Calendar of State Papers, Foreign

Calendar of State Papers, France

Calendar of State Papers, Scotland

Calendar of State Papers, Spain

Calendar of State Papers, Venice

Carte, Thomas, *A General History of England*, London, 1750

Cartwright, J., *Christina of Denmark Duchess of Milan and Lorraine*, London, 1913

Castor, Helen, *Blood and Roses*, London, 2004

Cavendish, George, *The Life and Death of Cardinal Wolsey*, Massachusetts, 1905

Childe-Pemberton, William S, *Elizabeth Blount and Henry the Eighth, with some account of her surroundings*, 1913

Cox, John, (ed.), *Miscellaneous Writings and Letters of Thomas Cranmer*, Cambridge, 1846

Cripps-Day, FH, *The History of the Tournament in England and France*, London, 1918

Denny, Joanna, *Anne Boleyn: A New Life of England's Tragic Queen*, London, 2004

Denny, Joanna: *Katherine Howard*, London, 2005

Dickens, A.G., *Thomas Cromwell and the English Reformation*, London, 1977

Dunkin, *The History and Antiquities of Dartford: With Topographical Notices of the Neighbourhood*, London, 1844

Erasmus, Desiderius, *The Collected Works of Erasmus*, vols 1-8, Toronto, 1974-1988

Erickson, Carolly, *Great Harry: The Extravagant Life of Henry VIII*, London, 1997

Everett Green, Mary Anne, *Lives of the Princesses of England from the Norman Conquest*, London, 1857

Everett Wood, Mary Anne, *Letters of Royal and Illustrious Ladies of Great Britain*, London, 1846

Freer, Martha Walker, *The Life of Jeanne d'Albret, Queen of Navarre*, Volume 1, London, 1855

Foxe, John, *Acts and Monuments (The Book of Martyrs)*, ed. Pratt, · London, 1874

Fraser, Antonia, *The Six Wives of Henry VIII*, London, 1992

Froude, James: *The Reign of Mary Tudor*, London, 1910

Garrett, Christina Hallowell: *The Marian Exiles*, Cambridge, 1938

Gee, H. and Hardy W J., (eds), *Documents Illustrative of English Church History*, London, 1914

Grafton, Richard, *Grafton's Chronicle, Or History of England: To which is Added His Table of the Bailiffs, Sheriffs and Mayors of the City of London from the Year 1189, to 1558, Volumes 1 and 2*, London, 1809

Griffiths, R A, *The Making of the Tudor Dynasty*, Stroud, 2011

Gunn, S. J., *Charles Brandon, Duke of Suffolk 1484–1545*, Oxford, 1988

Guy, John: *The Children of Henry VIII*, Oxford, 2013

Guy, John: *Tudor England*, Oxford, 1998

Hall, Edward, *Hall's Chronicle: Containing the history of England*, ed. H. Ellis, London, 1809

Hamilton, W.D., *Wriotheseley's Chronicle,* Camden Society, 1875

Hasler, PW (ed.): 'The Role of the Marian Exiles' in *The History of Parliament: the House of Commons 1558–1603*. Available from the History of Parliament Online

Hayward, Maria, *Dress at the Court of King Henry VIII*, London, 2017

Herbert, Edward, *The Life and Reign of King Henry VIII.: Together with a General History of Those Times*, London, 1740

Holinshed, Raphael, *Chronicles of England, Scotland and Ireland*, London, 1807

Hume, Martin Andrew Sharp, *The Wives of Henry the Eighth and the Parts They Played in History,* London, 1905

Ives, Eric, *Lady Jane Grey: A Tudor Mystery*, London, 2011

Ives, Eric, *The Life and Death of Anne Boleyn*, London, 2005

Kempe, Alfred (ed.), *The Loseley Manuscripts and other rare documents*, London, 1836

Koenigsberger, *Monarchies, States Generals and Parliaments: The Netherlands in the Fifteenth and Sixteenth Centuries*, Cambridge, 2001

Leland, *De Rebus Brittanicis Collectanea*, London, 1774

Letters and Papers, Foreign and Domestic, Henry VIII

Lindsey, K., *Divorced Beheaded Survived*, Reading, 1995

Loades, David, *Henry VIII: Court, church and conflict*, The National Archives, 2007

Loades, David, *Henry VIII: King and Court*, Andover, 2009

Loades, David: *Mary Tudor*, Oxford, 1989

Loades, David: *The Politics of Marriage: Henry VIII and his Queens*, Stroud, 1994

Mackay, Lauren, *Inside the Tudor Court*, Stroud, 2014

Mackray, W.D., *The Remonstrance of Anne of Cleves*, Archaeologia 47, 1883

Madden, F.W., *The Privy Purse Expenses of the Princess Mary December 1536 to December 1544*, London, 1831

Mathusiak, John, *Henry VIII*, Stroud, 2013

McConica, James, *English Humanists and Reformation Politics*, Oxford, 1968

McEntegart, Rory, *Henry VIII, The League of Schmalkalden and the English Reformation*, London, 2002

Merriman, RB, *Life and Letters of Thomas Cromwell*, Oxford, 1902

Morris, S., and Grueninger, N., *In the Footsteps of the Six Wives of Henry VIII*, Stroud, 2016

Nichols, John G, (ed.), *A Collection of ordinances and regulations for the government of the royal household, made in divers reigns from King Edward III to King William and Queen Mary*, 1790

Nichols, John G, (ed.), *The Chronicle of Calais, in the reigns of Henry VII and Henry VIII to the year 1540*, J. B. Nichols and Son, 1846

Nichols, John G, (ed.), *The Chronicle of Queen Jane and of Two Years of Queen Mary*, London, 1849

Nichols, John G, (ed.), *The Diary of Henry Machyn*, London, 1848

Norton, Elizabeth, *Anne of Cleves*, Stroud, 2010

Norton, Elizabeth: *England's Queens*, Stroud, 2012

Palmer, *A Treatise on the Church of Christ*, Oxford, 1838

Plowden, Alison, *Lady Jane Grey*, Stroud, 2004

Plowden, Alison, *The Young Elizabeth*, Stroud, 1971

Plowden, Alison, *Tudor Women*, London, 1979

Porter, Linda: *Mary Tudor: The First Queen*, London, 2007

Rank, Otto, *The Myth of the Birth of the Hero*, Maryland, 2004

Rappaport, Steve, *Worlds Within Worlds: Structures of Life in*

Sixteenth-Century London, Cambridge, 2002

Rex, Richard: *Henry VIII*, Stroud, 2009

Rex, Richard: *The Tudors*, Stroud, 2002

Richardson, Walter C, *Mary Tudor: The White Queen*, London, 1970

Ridley, Jasper: *Henry VIII*, London, 1984

Ridley, Jasper: *The Life and Times of Mary Tudor*, London, 1973

Ridley, Jasper: *The Tudor Age*, London, 1988

Ruddock, A., 'The Earliest Original English Seaman's Rutter and Pilot's Chart', *Journal of Navigation*, 14(4), 409-431, 1961

Saaler, Mary, *Anne of Cleves: Fourth Wife of Henry VIII*, London, 1995

Scarisbrick, J J, *Henry VIII*, London, 1997

Sharpe, Kevin, *Selling the Tudor Monarchy: Authority and Image in Sixteenth Century England*, Yale, 2009

Simpson, Leonard, *The Autobiography of the Emperor Charles V*, London, 1862

Skidmore, C., *Edward VI The Lost King of England*, London, 2007

Sim, Alison, *Food and Feast in Tudor England*, Stroud, 1997

Sim, Alison, *Masters and Servants in Tudor England*, Stroud, 2006

Smollett, T., *A Complete History of England*, London, 1757

Starkey, David, *Elizabeth: Apprenticeship*, London, 2001

Starkey, David, *Henry, Virtuous Prince*, London, 2009

Starkey, David, *The Reign of Henry VIII*, London, 1985

Starkey, David, *Six Wives: The Queens of Henry VIII*, London, 2003

St Clare Byrne, M., (ed.), *The Lisle Letters*, Chicago, 1981

Stow, John, *A Survey of London*, London. 1876

Strickland, Agnes, *Lives of the Queens of England*, London, 1844

Strype, *Ecclesiastical Memorials of Henry VIII, Edward VI and Mary*, London, 1816

The British and Foreign Review, Vol. 9, London, 1839

Thomas, A H and Thornley, I D, eds., *Great Chronicle of London*, London, 1938

Thurley, Simon: *The Palaces of Tudor England*, Yale, 1993

Trio, Paul and de Smet, Marjan, *The Use and Abuse of Sacred Places in Late Medieval Towns*, Leuven, 2006

Tytler, Sarah, *Tudor Queens and Princesses*, London, 1896

Vergil, Polydore, *Anglica Historia, A hypertext critical edition,* ed. Sutton, Dana F, Irvine, 2005

Walker, Williston, *History of the Christian Church*, London, 1985

Warnicke, Retha M., *The Marrying of Anne of Cleves: Royal Protocol in Tudor England*, Cambridge, 2000

Watkins, Sarah-Beth, *Lady Katherine Knollys: The Unacknowledged Daughter of King Henry VIII*, Winchester, 2014

Wernham, R. B., *Before the Armada: The Emergence of the English Nation, 1485-1588*, London, 1966

Weir, Alison, *The Six Wives of Henry VIII*, London, 1991

Weir, Alison, *Henry VIII: King and Court*, London, 2008

Wilkinson, Josephine, *Katherine Howard: The Tragic Story of Henry VIII's Fifth Queen*, London, 2016

Wilson, Derek, *Hans Holbein: Portrait of an Unknown Man*, London, 1996

Young, Alan, *Tudor and Jacobean Tournaments*, London, 1987

Chronos Books
HISTORY

Chronos Books is an historical non-fiction imprint. Chronos
publishes real history for real people; bringing to life people,
places and events in an imaginative, easy-to-digest and
accessible way - histories that pass on their stories to a
generation of new readers.
If you have enjoyed this book, why not tell other readers by
posting a review on your preferred book site.

Recent bestsellers from Chronos Books are:

Lady Katherine Knollys

The Unacknowledged Daughter of King Henry VIII

Sarah-Beth Watkins

A comprehensive account of Katherine Knollys' questionable paternity, her previously unexplored life in the Tudor court and her intriguing relationship with Elizabeth I.

Paperback: 978-1-78279-585-8 ebook: 978-1-78279-584-1

Cromwell was Framed

Ireland 1649

Tom Reilly

Revealed: The definitive research that proves the Irish nation owes Oliver Cromwell a huge posthumous apology for wrongly convicting him of civilian atrocities in 1649.

Paperback: 978-1-78279-516-2 ebook: 978-1-78279-515-5

Why The CIA Killed JFK and Malcolm X

The Secret Drug Trade in Laos

John Koerner

A new groundbreaking work presenting evidence that the CIA silenced JFK to protect its secret drug trade in Laos.

Paperback: 978-1-78279-701-2 ebook: 978-1-78279-700-5

The Disappearing Ninth Legion

A Popular History

Mark Olly

The Disappearing Ninth Legion examines hard evidence for the foundation, development, mysterious disappearance, or possible continuation of Rome's lost Legion.

Paperback: 978-1-84694-559-5 ebook: 978-1-84694-931-9

Beaten But Not Defeated

Siegfried Moos - A German anti-Nazi who settled in Britain
Merilyn Moos
Siegi Moos, an anti-Nazi and active member of the German
Communist Party, escaped Germany in 1933 and, exiled in
Britain, sought another route to the transformation
of capitalism.
Paperback: 978-1-78279-677-0 ebook: 978-1-78279-676-3

A Schoolboy's Wartime Letters

An evacuee's life in WWII — A Personal Memoir
Geoffrey Iley
A boy writes home during WWII, revealing his own fascinating
story, full of zest for life, information and humour.
Paperback: 978-1-78279-504-9 ebook: 978-1-78279-503-2

The Life & Times of the Real Robyn Hoode

Mark Olly
A journey of discovery. The chronicles of the genuine historical
character, Robyn Hoode, and how he became one of England's
greatest legends.
Paperback: 978-1-78535-059-7 ebook: 978-1-78535-060-3

Readers of ebooks can buy or view any of these bestsellers by clicking on the live link in the title. Most titles are published in paperback and as an ebook. Paperbacks are available in traditional bookshops. Both print and ebook formats are available online.

Find more titles and sign up to our readers' newsletter at
http://www.johnhuntpublishing.com/history-home

Follow us on Facebook at
https://www.facebook.com/ChronosBooks

and Twitter at https://twitter.com/ChronosBooks